Francia 799–911

COMBAT

Viking Warrior
VERSUS
Frankish Warrior

Noah Tetzner

Illustrated by Johnny Shumate

OSPREY PUBLISHING
Bloomsbury Publishing Plc
Kemp House, Chawley Park, Cumnor Hill, Oxford OX2 9PH, UK
29 Earlsfort Terrace, Dublin 2, Ireland
1385 Broadway, 5th Floor, New York, NY 10018, USA
E-mail: info@ospreypublishing.com
www.ospreypublishing.com

OSPREY is a trademark of Osprey Publishing Ltd

First published in Great Britain in 2022

A catalogue record for this book is available from the British Library.

ISBN: PB 9781472848857; eBook 9781472848833;
ePDF 9781472848840; XML 9781472848864

22 23 24 25 26   10 9 8 7 6 5 4 3 2 1

Maps by www.bounford.com
Index by Rob Munro
Typeset by PDQ Digital Media Solutions, Bungay, UK
Printed and bound in India by Replika Press Private Ltd.

Osprey Publishing supports the Woodland Trust, the UK's leading
woodland conservation charity.

To find out more about our authors and books visit
www.ospreypublishing.com. Here you will find extracts, author
interviews, details of forthcoming events and the option to sign up for
our newsletter.

Dedication

This book is dedicated to Andrew Gauerke, the man who introduced me
to Old Norse literature. Those pivotal weeks in which we read, together,
the Völsunga saga (Saga of the Volsungs) changed the course of my
destiny – spurring a lifelong interest in the medieval Viking world.

Author's acknowledgements

I would like to thank, most sincerely and gratefully, Dr Christian
Cooijmans. His guidance, support and unceasing enthusiasm helped
me write this book. I would also like to thank Dr Simon Coupland for
advising on the illustrations and providing an array of work that has
shaped scholarly knowledge of Frankish warriors during the Viking Age.
Finally, I wish to thank my editor Nick Reynolds, whose dedication and
expertise allowed this book to be published.

CONTENTS

INTRODUCTION   4

THE OPPOSING SIDES   10
Objectives and strategies • Command and leadership
Armies and warbands • Conduct in battle

THE FIRST CLASHES   31
799–840

THE GREAT ASSAULT   45
840–77

THE LATER RAIDS   60
877–911

ANALYSIS   71

AFTERMATH   75

BIBLIOGRAPHY   77

INDEX   80

Introduction

As the 8th century drew to a close, the formidable Frankish king known to posterity as Charlemagne (748–814; r. 768–814) ruled over a vast and expanding empire stretching from the Pyrenees to the borders of what is now Hungary. As Charlemagne's forces consolidated his overlordship in newly conquered Saxony and the Franks offered succour to Pope Leo III, restoring him to his throne in Rome, a small group of warriors raided the island of Noirmoutier on the Atlantic coast of what is now France, plundering the wealthy monastery of Saint-Philibert. The monks were taken violently by surprise, though a few of them escaped. A contingent of Frankish warriors, probably members of the coast guard or *lantweri* (local levy forces), met the Vikings in battle. According to Alcuin of York, a prominent scholar and one of Charlemagne's principal advisors, during raids on the coast of Aquitaine the defenders killed more than 100 of the raiders and destroyed some of their ships (Cooijmans 2020: 101). This statement from Alcuin is believed to denote the raid on Noirmoutier in 799, at least in part, as other islands were evidently affected by these early Viking incursions as well.

The Frankish monk Notker, known as 'the Stammerer', described in his work *Gesta Karoli* (The Deeds of Charles) a dramatic scene in which the Frankish king actually witnessed the raid on Noirmoutier. Notker tells us that having arrived at an unnamed coastal town in western Francia, Charlemagne sat eating his dinner when a fleet of Scandinavian pirates assaulted the harbour. At first, there was much confusion among the Franks as to the identity of these marauders. Some thought them to be Jewish merchants and others declared that they were traders from distant Africa or neighbouring Britain. Charlemagne, however, instantly recognized them as Northmen from the build of their longships and the speed at which they moved through the water. As the Vikings withdrew from the harbour, contingents of Charlemagne's men pursued them, but were quickly outsailed. Notker explains that Charlemagne then rose from the table and stood at a window facing east. For a long time,

tears poured down his face. No one dared to ask him why. In the end, the Frankish king spoke, saying that he was not afraid of harm the Vikings could do to him but wept in foresight of the damage they would bring upon his descendants and their subjects.

While Notker's story is a fable, it certainly implies the Frankish king's early recognition of the destruction the Northmen would wreak upon his legacy. While this first recorded Viking raid on Francia ended in defeat for the raiders, it presaged a growing threat to the mighty empire ruled by Charlemagne and his heirs. As the 9th century progressed, the Vikings' raids would grow in size and scale and threaten the integrity of the Frankish lands, with major cities such as Rouen, Rheims, Hamburg, Aachen and even Paris falling prey to the Northmen's assault.

Even before the Noirmoutier raid, Charlemagne and his counsellors were already aware of the emerging threat posed by the Vikings. Six years earlier, in 793, a Viking warband attacked and plundered the monastery of Lindisfarne off the coast of Northumbria. News of the attack spread swiftly, reaching Charlemagne's court by the end of that year. Alcuin wrote to the surviving monks of Lindisfarne, offering condolences and expressing the outrage felt among Christians across Carolingian Europe.

Alcuin's communication with the monks of Lindisfarne suggests early contact between the Vikings and Franks. In his letter he suggested that Charlemagne might secure the return of 'boys' (possibly aristocratic children offered to the monastery by their parents) carried off as hostages by the Viking marauders, probably to Denmark (Nelson 1997: 21). Regarding the destruction brought upon the monastery of Lindisfarne, Alcuin famously

Detail from a 9th-century ivory casket from Metz, France, depicting a Frankish king on a throne and his soldiers and courtiers. The Viking depredations in Francia would test the Frankish apparatus of state to the limits, with endemic civil war and long-running conflicts with neighbouring peoples such as the Bretons making the warfare of the period especially endemic. (DeAgostini/Getty Images)

OPPOSITE
An early pirate incursion on the Frankish coast was witnessed by a monk named Albinus (aka Aubin), who went on to become the bishop of Angers in the 6th century. Canonized, he became the patron saint of those praying for protection against pirate attack. This illustration of warriors in transit, appearing in *The Life of Saint-Aubin*, can be dated to about 1100. (Art Images via Getty Images)

condemned the pagan invaders; to this day, his words have conjured the enduring image of ferocious heathen warriors, responsible for beginning an age of violence; but while the Vikings burned, captured, slaughtered and pillaged, the Franks themselves were notorious for their violent methods of asserting military dominance. In 782, for example, Charlemagne executed 4,500 Saxons at Verdun, proving that Christian Franks could be just as brutal as their pagan adversaries from Scandinavia. For more than a century, the two sides' fighting men would confront one another in a host of encounters, from the borders of Denmark to the heart of the Frankish Empire, as opportunistic raiding gave way to occupation, extortion and siege warfare.

Plunder and profit were the chief motivations for the Vikings' activities in Francia in the 9th century. These gold coins, dating from the Charlemagne era and minted in France in the 9th century, are displayed at the Geldmuseum (Money Museum) of the German Central Bank in Frankfurt. (Horacio Villalobos/Corbis via Getty Images)

While Greek and Roman authors coined the term 'Scandinavia' (Parker 2014: 18), the peoples of what are now Denmark, Norway and Sweden only emerged into prominence in the years following the Lindisfarne raid of 793. Our understanding of the many cultures that inhabited the region comes from archaeological finds and the careful interpretation of the surviving literary sources. What is clear is that during the Vendel Period, as the 250 years before 790 are called, Scandinavia was inhabited by a variety of Germanic clans which were constantly at war with one another. Although it is not possible to establish the identities of the rulers of these peoples, it is clear that during the 650s and possibly even earlier, rulers in Denmark were capable of directing the construction of an enormous structure known as the Danevirke. While this took on the properties of a defensive barrier some 30km long, it seems that at the outset it was a shipping canal linking the Baltic Sea and the North Sea, via the Schlei Inlet and the rivers Treene and Eider. By the early 9th century, the Danevirke had become a defensive structure.

By the beginning of the Viking Age, Scandinavia was a patchwork of small kingdoms ruled by minor chieftains who warred among themselves and forged alliances, and entered into federations. The concentration of power gradually expanded as stronger kingdoms absorbed smaller ones in an uneven process of 'state-building'. Royal power did not develop uniformly throughout Scandinavia as political situations varied throughout the many independent regions. The kingdom of Denmark developed early, and the Danes' geographical and economic advantages allowed them to dominate much of Scandinavia through overlordship for much of the Viking Age. While Danish control over some of the more northern regions did not amount to anything more than the recognition of Danish kings as overlords, they rarely intervened in the administrations of territories beyond what was then defined as Denmark.

In 799, the Franks were at the height of their power and influence, but they had been a force in European affairs for hundreds of years. The Merovingian dynasty emerged in the 5th century and continued until 751, when Childeric III (c.717–c.754; r. 743–51) was deposed and Pepin (714–68; r. 751–68), known as 'the Short', was crowned king of the Franks. Pepin's son Charles initially shared the Frankish realm with his brother Carloman I (751–71; r. 768–71), the latter's death allowing Charlemagne to reunite the empire under a single ruler. Like the Merovingians, the Carolingians divided inheritances among heirs, meaning that when a monarch died, his lands were divided among his legitimate male offspring; this practice was enshrined in law, and would engender much disorder and bloodshed as eligible heirs competed to defend and supplement their inheritance.

While many scholars place special significance on the Lindisfarne raid in 793, it was certainly not the first time the coast of western Europe had been attacked by raiders from the sea. Though irregular, several reports of Scandinavian attacks on the European continent pre-date the Carolingian Age itself. One such account, related by the Frankish bishop, Gregory of Tours, described an attack along the northern coast of the early 6th-century Merovingian realm, in which a Danish warband had come ashore and laid waste to a Frankish village and taken captives (Cooijmans 2020: 100).

As the Franks pushed north and east, they also came into contact with the Scandinavians on their home territory. Another encounter is related in the work of the Merovingian court poet, Venantius Fortunatus, who wrote about a Frankish clash with the Saxon and Danish peoples near the River Bordaa, possibly today's River Boorne in northern Frisia (Cooijmans 2020: 101). This particularly early battle between Franks, Saxons and Danes has been dated to the late 6th century.

During the late 7th century the Franks combined their efforts to build a territorial empire with the propagation of Christianity (Collins 1999: 255). Accordingly, Frankish monasteries sent missionaries into Frisia, the marshy territory between the Rhine and the North Sea, as Francia's political leadership sought to make Frisia a Frankish client state. When the Frisians intervened in a Frankish civil war in the 710s, the victorious Frankish faction turned on the Frisians and defeated them at the battle of the Boam in 734; western Frisia was conquered by the Franks, with the eastern part following in 785.

Charlemagne fought a series of campaigns to expand his patrimony. It began with the annexation of northern Italy, in which he was crowned King of the Lombards on 10 July 774. He then moved into Spain and entrusted his third legitimate son, Louis (778–840), called 'the Pious', with securing the Spanish March. Bavaria was subsequently incorporated into the Frankish Empire in 788, and the Avars, a nomadic people who ruled an empire on both sides of the River Danube, were defeated in 788–96. While Charlemagne's armies swept across Europe, the Frankish king's greatest struggle was against a Germanic people who inhabited the land just south of Denmark. The Saxons, the Franks' north-eastern neighbours, stoutly resisted Charlemagne's armies for 32 years from 772. A Frisian uprising was crushed in 793, and by 799, Frisia appeared to be firmly under Frankish rule as the Frankish border approached that of Denmark.

Paradoxically, Charlemagne's success in expanding his empire and pacifying Frisia left the region open to Danish attack. While the Franks effectively supplanted the Frisians in terms of the lucrative trade conducted from ports such as Quentovic and Dorestad, Charlemagne's men lacked the maritime expertise to counter the Danes at sea.

Frankish territory in 768
Charlemagne's conquests
Danish territories

Birka

Kaupang

North Sea

Lindisfarne

Ribe

Hedeby

Reric

York

Hamburg

Obotrites

FRISIA

Bremen

SAXONY

Veleti

Oder

Dorestad

Rhine

Elbe

London

Winchester

Channel

St Omer

Tournai

St Amand

Cologne

Sorbs

Fulda

THURINGIA

Quentovic

Aachen

St Vaast

Prüm

Mainz

Czechs

St Riquier

Tertry

Trier

Corbie

Jumièges

Rouen

AUSTRASIA

Rheims

Metz

Verdun

Regensburg

Danube

Moravians

Paris

Seine

SWABIA

NEUSTRIA

Sens

Strasbourg

Bretons

Luxeuil

BAVARIA

Salzburg

Tours

Loire

St Gall

CARINTHIA

Avars

NOIRMOUTIER

Nantes

BURGUNDY

Poitiers

Geneva

Lyon

Milan

Venice

Croats

Vienne

AQUITAINE

Pavia

Po

Bordeaux

Rhône

LOMBARDY

Ravenna

Serbs

GASCONY

Toulouse

SEPTIMANIA

Arles

PROVENCE

Narbonne

N

Mediterranean

Corsicans

Spoleto

SPANISH MARCH

Ebro

0   200 miles

0   200km

Rome

The Opposing Sides

OBJECTIVES AND STRATEGIES

One of the most intriguing aspects of the struggle between the Franks and the Vikings in the 9th and early 10th centuries is the wide gulf between the two sides' objectives. While the Vikings were interested in trading and the acquisition of plunder and slaves and did not wish to pursue a war of conquest, the Franks were determined to eject the raiders and protect the cities, religious houses and farms of Francia.

This picture was made more complex by the complicated relationships between competing Frankish factions and among the Vikings themselves, and the presence of other parties such as the Bretons, who enjoyed an ambivalent relationship with the Northmen. The situation evolved as parties of Vikings decided to establish temporary settlements to facilitate their raiding activities and then subsequently resolved to settle permanently in the area around Rouen, and the Frankish regimes were forced to accommodate the Northmen in the long-term politics of West Francia.

In their efforts to prevent Viking raids on Frankish territory, the Carolingian regimes – particularly those of Charlemagne and Louis the Pious (778–840; r. 814–40) – sought to exert diplomatic, military and even religious pressure on the Danish realm. Periods of Danish civil war and unrest within that kingdom tended to reduce the number of Northmen seeking to make their fortunes through raiding, as Danes and other Scandinavians were diverted by the need to defend their own homes and fight for position and influence among their countrymen. Conversely, when Denmark was ruled firmly by its shadowy kings, the number of potential raiders increased as warriors and traders, thwarted at home, sought to prosper through raiding in Francia instead. When Frankish diplomacy failed, or when the Danish crown was able to assert its power, the Frankish lands were subjected to greater pressure from Viking raiders.

Viking

The Viking raiding parties that sought to wrest loot and slaves from Francia were aided by their innovative maritime technology and the apparent absence of a political agenda. While Vikings often avoided open battle with Frankish armies, they enacted a scorched-earth policy, destroying much in their wake. There was considerable damage to property, and food and resources were taken by force; but given sufficient warning, monastic communities could move their valuables and libraries to other locations for safekeeping (Coupland & Nelson 1988: 8). The leaders of these raiding expeditions were primarily interested in plunder and in keeping their followers fed and supplied.

As well as building up a detailed picture of the physical geography of the Frankish realm, the Viking raiding parties developed a sophisticated understanding of Frankish habits and idiosyncrasies, allowing the Northmen to target vulnerable communities on key dates in the calendar, such as saint's days, when markets would attract Frankish traders and customers to major settlements. The longship was the key factor in the Northmen's favour, giving the raiders the range to reach vulnerable targets and the speed with which to evade pursuit.

While longships were sturdy and capable of sailing through oceans and shallow waters alike, they were not invulnerable to major storms. Although the combination of oar and sail meant that the Vikings could brave challenging weather, their longships were no match for the mightiest gales of coastal regions. At Noirmoutier, a tidal island and site of the first Viking raid on Francia, the Scandinavians are believed to have been shipwrecked, probably because of the low and subsequently rising tides (Cooijmans 2020: 101). The Northmen's success in ranging more widely along Francia's coastline – and inland via the many rivers that criss-crossed the Frankish lands – was dependent upon the acquisition of knowledge of local conditions; given the absence of maps, Viking

Dragon heads similar to this one, preserved at the Vikingskipshuset (Viking Ship Museum) in Bygdøy, Norway, adorned the forepart of a longship's prow. During the Viking Age, longships were both the Northmen's primary transport method and an iconic symbol of their power. Scandinavian shipbuilders attempted to combine lightness with strength and flexibility, using carefully selected timber for construction. Those longships that have been found were built of oak. These warships were low and narrow relative to their length and featured a deck that ran the entire length of the ship. Oar-ports were located along the sides, their number making it possible to estimate the crew of each ship (Roesdahl 2016: 89). By way of shield-battens, shields could be placed along the outer sides of a longship, this being an iconic feature of the Viking warship (Roesdahl 2016: 90). (Maurice ROUGEMONT/Gamma-Rapho via Getty Images)

This well-born Viking is eager to gain plunder and social standing in the raids on Francia. His wealthy background provides him with the perfect opportunity to seek a career as a warrior. He has undergone extensive military training and is able to pay the high cost of his weapons and armour. This warrior is likely to feel safe in the isolated forest and marshland of Louvain, protecting him from Frankish cavalry manoeuvres. Having constructed a surrounding ditch and motivated by the recent forays into the surrounding area, there is no reason why this Viking did not assume there would be an easy victory, should a Frankish force engage his camp.

Weapons, dress and equipment

This warrior prepares to strike a blow with his sword (**1**), a Frankish blade bearing the trademark inscription 'Ulfberht'. The 9th century saw the development of inlaid inscriptions on sword blades; the oldest known Ulfberht blade dates from about 800, although such blades continued to be crafted over the following three centuries. In addition to his sword, this warrior carries a type of knife called a *seax* (**2**), which doubled as a tool and was ideal for the closest of combat encounters.

The quantity of metal and labour involved in crafting mail (**3**) made it a luxury item, probably more expensive than a sword. Mail was flexible, though heavy, and was intended to protect a warrior from cutting or slicing actions in addition to absorbing some of the impact from hostile blows. Mail alone did little to protect against heavily concentrated blows as these would drive the metal rings

into the wearer's body. Mail needed to be worn atop a padded garment such as a stuffed coat. This combination would have been heavy and hot, however, undoubtedly affecting a warrior's stamina and morale.

The standard Viking helmet (**4**) appears to be of a conical design with a nasal guard. This piece of armour protected the upper portion of the head, an ideal target for enemy blows and arrow shots. While this helmet is made of metal, others would be made of boiled leather, in which case they would be lighter and cooler to wear while still providing some protection. A round wooden shield (**5**) protects this warrior from the lower face to his upper legs. Viking shields were similar to those of the Franks in design and encompassed a central metal boss, likely bearing metal or leather rims. He also carries a leather pouch (**6**) for coins or personal items.

The Oseberg ship, excavated in 1904–05 and now displayed at the Viking Ship Museum, is pierced for 15 oars on each side; it was probably a hybrid of a warship and a trading ship. Longships were steered by means of a large oar placed near the stern on the right-hand side of the vessel. As well as their oars, longships were propelled by a square sail, which could be reefed, reducing the sail area in strong wind. No Viking Age sails have ever been recovered intact; they are known to have been woven by women (Friðriksdóttir 2020: 82). Modern testing has indicated that longships could maintain an average speed of 4–5 knots with the use of oars, but could increase their speed to 9 knots for short periods of time. Under sail, the speed could be increased to as much as 20 knots, depending on the conditions. The speed of travel and the range afforded to the Vikings by way of their longships gave them a key tactical advantage over the Franks and was critically important in several situations such as pursuit or flight from the enemy. The Vikings' use of sails enabled them to traverse long stretches of water. Had they relied solely on oars, journeys from Scandinavia would have no doubt been hard on the Vikings' stamina and morale. The combination of sails (which afforded range) and oars (which provided speed) made the Vikings exceptionally deadly as they could traverse Frankish waterways relatively without issue. (Omar Marques/Anadolu Agency/Getty Images)

leaders would rely on hard-earned information about the peculiarities of each coastal region. Such knowledge was doubtless built on the activities of Danish traders in the preceding years (Nelson 1997: 22). This may have contributed to the recurrent patterns of raiding evident in the Viking Age, as the Northmen returned to familiar locations on multiple occasions.

No seafaring warband could remain on the move forever. The building of encampments allowed the Scandinavians to combat hunger, fatigue and low morale; damaged ships could be repaired and new ones constructed. The *Annals of Saint-Bertin*, a Frankish chronicle intended to continue the *Royal Frankish Annals*, state that in 862, a company of Vikings at Jumièges opted to repair their ships and wait for spring (Nelson 1991: 98), while another fleet on the River Seine beached their vessels at a place suitable for repairing ships and constructing new ones in 866 (Cooijmans 2020: 141).

Viking encampments were often built on or near the banks of navigable rivers. Parties of Northmen were also known to establish themselves on islands within these waterways (Cooijmans 2020: 142). By setting up camp at the water's edge, Vikings retained the ability to fall back on their ships should their positions become vulnerable to Frankish attacks. Constructed in naturally defensible locations, these encampments often relied on man-made fortifications to keep adversaries at bay. For example, the Viking camp at Louvain in 891 was reportedly enclosed with a rampart and palisade. Surviving written sources suggest that such camps were traditionally built in a semicircular fashion; ramparts seem to have been made of earth, stone and wood, often topped with palisades and surrounded by ditches and stakes (Cooijmans 2020: 143).

In addition to building their own fortifications, Vikings captured Frankish settlements for defensive purposes. Regino of Prüm, an East Frankish monk and chronicler, describes how the Vikings occupied the city of Angers and rebuilt its defences; in 873, Viking use of the fortified centre of Angers initially prevented the West Frankish king Charles (823–77; r. 843–77), known as 'the Bald', from successfully investing the city. The palace of Nijmegen in Frisia served a similar purpose; Louis the Younger could not surmount local Viking fortifications when besieging Nijmegen in 880.

Written sources attest that Vikings also occupied monasteries, though their efficiency as defensive structures has been questioned by scholars. Nevertheless, the monk Abbo described part of his own abbey at Saint-Germain being used by Scandinavians during the siege of Paris in 886. He wrote that the Vikings had set up their camps and constructed ramparts across the field at his monastery.

Having established encampments throughout the Frankish realm, Vikings did not remain within their confines. Encampments were more than places of rest and refuge; these were the sites of assembly, departure and withdrawals. Little is known about the Vikings' strategic mobility once on land, but it seems that the horse was a key factor in their activities, affording the raiders vital speed and flexibility. As the Vikings tended to operate in small-scale warbands or companies, it may be assumed that they had superior mobility on land when compared to their Frankish adversaries. Small, agile warbands could then, if necessary, link up with other groups of warriors to form larger contingents and achieve a common goal.

Frankish

In response to the ever-growing threat of Viking raiders, the Frankish defenders implemented three complementary military countermeasures: direct engagement, containment and fortification. The Frankish warriors opposing the Northmen were drawn from three overlapping categories: the coast guard, the *lantweri* and the royal host.

The initial line of Frankish defence against the Scandinavians, both at sea and on land, was provided by the coast guard. Beginning in 800, the Viking threat meant that the Frankish coastline facing the North Sea, the Channel and the Atlantic Ocean was placed under close watch (Coupland 2004: 50). According to the *Royal Frankish Annals*, all of Francia's North Sea ports and navigable river mouths were guarded by contingents of warriors. After a Danish fleet attacked Frisia in 810, Charlemagne ordered the construction of ships and increased security measures, while the coast guard was placed on high alert. On land, the coast guard kept watch for seafaring raiders and defended the shore if such raiders attempted a land invasion. In the case of a seaborne threat, some type of signalling network was employed to coordinate the Frankish response, but it is unclear how this functioned (Coupland 2004: 50).

This detail, taken from the bible commissioned by Count Vivian of Tours in 845 and presented to Charles the Bald in 846, shows St Jerome leaving Rome for Jerusalem. Although the Franks undoubtedly built ships – indeed, they deployed fleets against Arab raiders in the south – there is no indication that they harnessed the full potential of naval power to oppose the Vikings in the North Sea (Coupland 2004: 50). What few ships the Franks did have were used to create local flotillas along the coasts, near river mouths and in harbours. The coast guard's lack of a proper naval force would enable Viking fleets to come and go as they pleased. If a Viking raiding party spotted a contingent of the Frankish coast guard on land, the Northmen could simply sail away and raid a less-defended location. (Leemage/ Corbis via Getty Images)

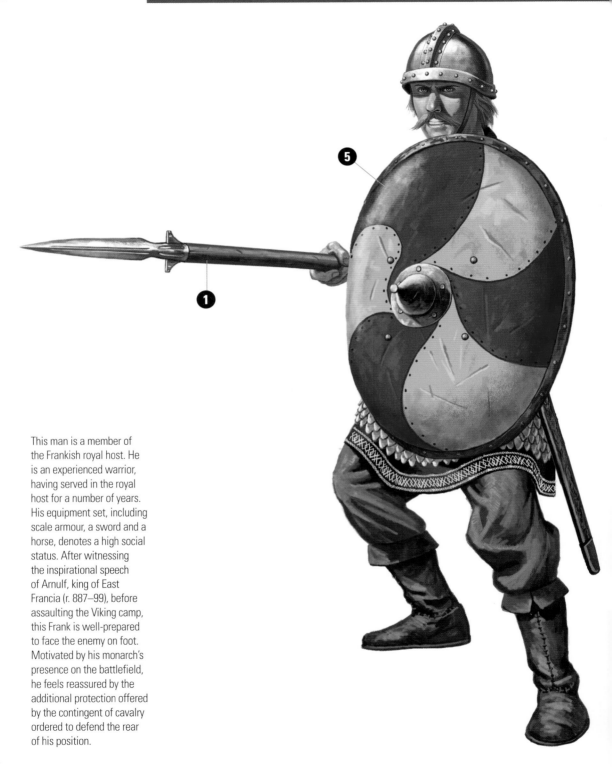

This man is a member of the Frankish royal host. He is an experienced warrior, having served in the royal host for a number of years. His equipment set, including scale armour, a sword and a horse, denotes a high social status. After witnessing the inspirational speech of Arnulf, king of East Francia (r. 887–99), before assaulting the Viking camp, this Frank is well-prepared to face the enemy on foot. Motivated by his monarch's presence on the battlefield, he feels reassured by the additional protection offered by the contingent of cavalry ordered to defend the rear of his position.

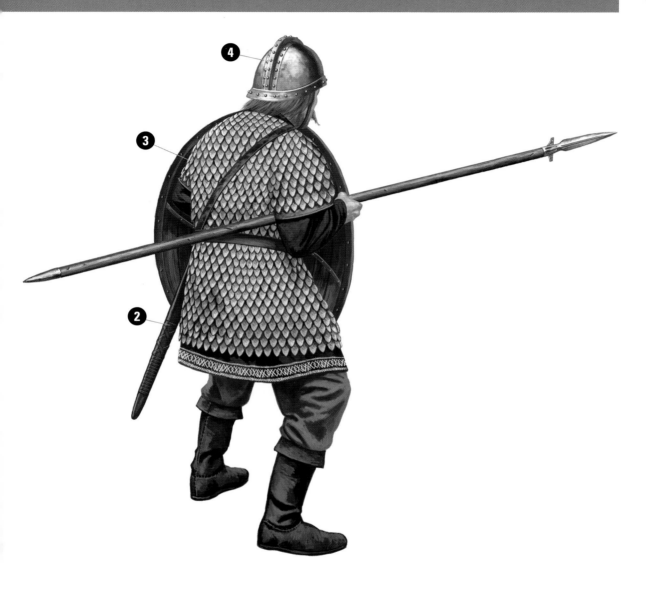

Weapons, dress and equipment

The *lancea* or spear (**1**), a cheap weapon available to any fighting man, was used by infantry and cavalry alike. Surviving textual sources suggest the Franks employed spears mainly as thrusting weapons, as this man is doing. This Frank also carries a *spata* or long sword (**2**), with a double-edged blade 80cm in length. Like the Viking, this man bears a blade with the inscription 'Ulfberht'.

During the reign of Charlemagne, those who owned large amounts of land were required to own a *brunia* or set of body armour (**3**), and any man who failed to bring his body armour on a campaign was stripped of it (Coupland 1990). A particular type of helmet (**4**) appears in Carolingian illustrations and resembles a slanted bowl attached to a neck guard with a prominent rim encircling the helmet.

Aside from his helmet and *brunia*, this Frank is protected by a wooden shield (**5**). In combat, the primary role of the shield was to ward off hostile blows and provide cover against ranged weapons. While this is undoubtedly true, the combination of a wooden shield and a curved metal boss enabled the shield to become an offensive weapon that the warrior could thrust into an enemy.

These two details depicting the Horsemen of the Apocalypse are taken from a 9th-century *Book of Revelation* associated with Saint-Amand Abbey; one detail shows two riders with slung shields and spears, while the other shows an archer on horseback. Note the use of stirrups and spurs, and the apparent absence of body armour and helmets. The shield was the cheapest piece of defensive equipment available to any Frankish warrior (Coupland 1990); while the sword was priced at five *solidi* in the *Lex Ribuaria*, a 7th-century collection of Frankish law, the shield and spear together cost a man just two *solidi*. It is clear from written and pictorial evidence that both infantry and cavalry regularly used the bow in combat. Sources from 802 and 806 state that each infantryman was expected to bring a bow with him on active service, along with a spare string and 12 arrows (Coupland 1990). This likely represents the contents of one quiver, which was slung across a warrior's back, attached by a strap and made of wood or leather. (DEA/G. DAGLI ORTI/Getty Images)

By the 830s, Viking raids in Frisia and Aquitaine were becoming increasingly successful, an indication that the Frankish coast guard was no longer effective. This may have been due to the increased size of Viking fleets or, as one chronicler suggested, the cowardice of the aristocracy who prepared to run rather than fight and were thoroughly terrified (Coupland 2004: 52). It should be noted that the Frankish troops' apparent ineffectiveness stemmed less from their availability and willingness to fight and more from their slow assemblage, limited mobility and occasional lack of discipline.

Accordingly, the Franks moved to a policy of containment, with mixed results. During the 840s, Charles the Bald attempted to counter the Vikings' penetration of West Francia's major rivers by stationing Frankish troops along the riverbanks to forestall a landing by the raiders. This tactic failed on the Seine in 845 when the Northmen launched a surprise attack on the south bank of the river and routed their landbound opponents (Coupland 2004: 63). It seems that this approach could succeed only if Frankish rivercraft were also available, as the Vikings could not so easily move past any waiting troops; this approach was made to work by Burchard, bishop of Chartres, and Agius, bishop of Orléans, in 854 on the River Loire. In 864, however, Lothair II, king of Lotharingia (r. 855–69), attempted to mount an amphibious assault on a Viking-held island in the River Rhine, but the Franks refused to press home the attack and it was called off (Coupland 2004: 64). As Coupland points out, complex combined operations of this type depended on a high degree of motivation, resilience and expertise among the Frankish forces entrusted with carrying them out, having surrendered the initiative to the raiders and often in the face of being locally outnumbered (Coupland 2004: 64).

The Franks' containment policy did succeed at Isles-lès-Villenoy in 862, however, when they successfully blocked a bridge over the River Marne while troops gathered along the riverbank, thereby compelling the Northmen to negotiate. Encouraged by this success and seeking to exclude the raiders permanently from the upper reaches of the Seine, Charles the Bald directed that the bridge at Pont-de-l'Arche be fortified, but in 865 the Vikings were aided by Frankish disorganization and timidity (Coupland 2004: 64). On the Loire, Les Ponts-de-Cé, south of Angers, was similarly fortified in the early 870s; it is notable that the surviving sources make no mention of Viking attacks along the upper reaches of the Loire after the completion of this building work in 873 (Coupland & Nelson 1988: 6). Even so, the containment strategy was discarded after Charles the Bald's death in 877.

Although Frankish coastal defences proved largely ineffective in the years after the death of Louis the Pious in 840, the ensuing decades bore witness to the renewal of coastal and inland fortifications in response to the Viking threat. Diocesan towns, among the principal Viking targets, seem to have been a key priority for Frankish reinforcement during the second half of the 9th century. Additionally, a number of enclosing Frankish fortifications have been attested archaeologically. The overall performance of such Frankish defences seems to have been favourable. The defences of Paris were sufficient to allow the garrison to keep a Viking army that outnumbered them at bay for many months in 885–86. Likewise, the walls of Saint-Bertin Abbey at Saint-Omer aided the Frankish defenders in their efforts to ward off a force of intruders in 891.

Charles the Bald reigned as king of West Francia during 843–77. His rule was defined by a constant struggle against Viking raiders and witnessed the sacking of Paris in 845. To counter Scandinavian raids, Charles sought to employ a defensive network of fortified bridges to block off major Frankish waterways and limit Viking mobility. These bridges were occasionally successful but inconvenienced Frankish commerce and trading vessels that could no longer sail along the vital waterways that had been blockaded. Charles's policy of containment followed in the footsteps of Charlemagne, who developed a network of coastal defences to protect his empire. (Archiv Gerstenberg/ullstein bild via Getty Images)

Some Frankish leaders resorted to handing over tribute to see off the Viking threat. Although contemporaries and subsequent commentators alike have seen the payment of *danegeld* as a disastrous, short-sighted expedient that simply stored up troubles for the future, the delivery of tribute does seem to have bought the Franks time to develop alternative strategies to combat the Scandinavian threat. In the case of Charles the Bald, for example, none of the Danish contingents whom he paid are known to have returned to his kingdom. Charles the Fat's decision to pay tribute only after months of siege warfare in 885–86 had exhausted his rival Odo (see page 65) severely damaged the Frankish king's reputation, but can be seen as a bid to have the Northmen eliminate a political rival that backfired when Odo survived and his personal standing was enhanced by his heroic efforts to defend Paris.

Finally, while the majority of the Franks wished to expel the Vikings from their territory, it should be borne in mind that some actually benefited from the Northmen's presence on Frankish soil, especially in times of civil war. The Northmen provided some Frankish leaders with highly mobile contingents of mercenaries, who could be used to attack neighbouring Frankish territories or other groups such as the Bretons amid the power struggles of the increasingly divided Carolingian Empire.

COMMAND AND LEADERSHIP

In this period, personal leadership on the battlefield was primarily a matter of leading by example. Warriors, whether Viking or Frankish, expected their leaders to fight in their midst and to share the risks of battle. Once battle was joined, it is likely that in most cases, the leaders of warbands would have conveyed instructions to their followers by the use of standards and musical instruments. Such methods were the only way to cut through the din and confusion of battle.

Viking

Any Scandinavian warrior seeking to make a name for himself had to build a tight-knit group of armed men upon whom he could rely. Swedish historian Anders Winroth notes (2012: 45) that it was not sufficient simply to pay one's followers, as codes of honour would have precluded such a relationship. Instead, potential associates had to be motivated to offer their support voluntarily. Alongside members of one's immediate family, other warriors could be brought into such an association by cultivating personal ties of mutual loyalty, cemented and reinforced by the giving and receiving of gifts. Such gifts, moreover, needed to be as prestigious and distinctive as possible; this informed the Vikings' targeting of particular forms of portable wealth, such as high-quality weapons, rather than simply seeking to amass large quantities of coinage or other tradeable assets (Winroth 2012: 45). It was generally understood that the nature and perceived value of the gift reflected the status of the giver and the recipient, and the value both parties placed on the relationship between the two.

The endemic conflict among warring Scandinavian chieftains occurred on the European continent as well as in the Viking homelands, and could be intense in periods of heightened tension with other peoples. The *Royal*

These 9th-century swords were found in Skiringssal, also known as Kaupang, one of Norway's first market towns. The example on the left has been ritually damaged. Viking swords were usually quite heavy, and while this weight enhanced the sword's thrusting and cutting power, it made changing the direction of an attack more difficult (Williams 2019: 16). Such swords had a point significant enough that they could be used as thrusting weapons, though they were primarily used for cutting. Both single- and double-edged blades are known to have been used by the Vikings in combat, though single-edged blades are largely restricted to the earlier portion of the Viking Age. (PHAS/Universal Images Group via Getty Images)

Dating from the 9th–11th centuries, these intricately decorated swords were discovered in Jutland, Denmark. Unlike spears and axes, Viking swords required large amounts of metal in their manufacture, making even the most basic examples fairly high-status items (Williams 2019: 14). Scandinavian swords were pattern-welded, the blades being crafted with several pieces of metal rather than just one. This metal-working technique was both time-consuming and costly, adding extra prestige to a weapon that was already of high value (Williams 2019: 19). Imported Frankish blades were common among the Vikings, and the Rhineland seems to have been an important centre for Frankish swordsmiths. Frankish sword blades have been discovered across the regions traversed by the Vikings, sometimes combined with locally crafted hilts, suggesting that blades were traded as sword components. In other surviving examples, the entire sword is of Frankish origin. On some occasions, Frankish swords may have been won by Vikings on the battlefield as a warrior without much wealth of his own might hope to gain one of these highly valuable objects from a fallen warrior no longer in need of it. (DEA/G. DAGLI ORTI/Getty Images)

Frankish Annals, during their account of the 810 frontier confrontation between Charlemagne and Godfred, king of the Danes, states that Godfred was killed by one of his own retinue (see page 36); in the warfare that ensued, multiple war leaders fought among themselves. Winroth observes that while it is tempting to see such struggles as a fight for the succession, this is to apply the standards and norms of other societies and times to early-9th-century Denmark. Power in Scandinavia, however, even in the relatively 'European' context of Denmark, was more about individual martial prowess and personal charisma than about lineage and inheritance (Winroth 2012: 44).

Frankish

Although the king acted as the Frankish forces' commander-in-chief, the mustering of forces and mobilization were organized by regional magnates. Counts were the primary mobilizing authorities for their own vassals and for free men owing military service. In addition to counts, bishops, abbots, abbesses, royal vassals and other lords could be responsible for mobilization. The first step in such a process was the assembly of lists recording how many men in each district were liable for conscription. Magnates also commanded sub-units on campaign (Coupland 2004: 59).

While the Frankish monarch was the supreme military commander and wielded much influence over the assembly and direction of an army, he was in the final analysis dependent on the magnates who led the contingents within it. If such figures did not discharge their obligations effectively – whether involuntarily or deliberately – disaster could ensue. The Frankish army could break up, not only leaving local communities vulnerable to Viking attack but also to the lasting detriment of royal authority. Where Frankish magnates changed sides, an imposing royal host could melt away; in 858 the Franks abandoned the blockade of a Viking camp on the Seine because numerous lords transferred their allegiance from Charles the Bald to his brother Louis (c.806–76), known as 'the German', the first king of East Francia (r. 843–76) (Coupland 2004: 60).

ARMIES AND WARBANDS

The size of Viking and Frankish armies is an ambiguous subject. Figures in contemporary sources ought to be read with caution, as they are almost always round numbers and sometimes contradict sources referring to the same army. For example, as Coupland notes, 500 Danes were killed with their leader Rodulf in 873, according to the *Annals of Saint-Bertin* and the *Annals of Xanten*, while the *Annals of Fulda* claim that the number of Vikings killed was 800 (Coupland 2004: 58). Realistically, Viking armies numbering in the hundreds (or thousands on significant occasions) seem to be congruent with contemporary accounts of Viking activity. Similarly, Frankish forces varied in strength, and detachments or individual contingents could operate independently of the royal host.

One must remember that neither the Franks nor the Vikings were unified among themselves. As civil war raged across the Frankish realm, local levies separated or distant from the royal host were often expected to defend themselves. Similarly, Vikings fought in small groups of warriors and only collaborated with other Scandinavians when a common goal was sought.

Viking

Two primary categories of professional Scandinavian warriors appear in historical and literary sources (Williams 2019: 28). The first category was composed of the *hirðmaðr* (household warriors) of a lord, chieftain or king. As members of a *hirð*, these warriors provided loyalty and military service to their warlord, whether they originated from his region or elsewhere, in exchange for provision and generosity. The generosity of a lord could be expressed in the form of necessities such as food and lodging or through expensive gifts such as arm rings made of silver and gold or ornate weapons that indicated the high status of both the warrior and his lord. Winroth notes the intricate relationship between Scandinavian warriors and their lords, resting upon the reciprocity and mutual obligations engendered by the giving and receiving of gifts, loyalty and military service (Winroth 2012: 10).

The second category of professional Scandinavian warriors was the *félag* (fellowship of warriors). This term appears in runic inscriptions of the Viking Age and may indicate the members of a trading venture or military company. The *Annals of Saint-Bertin* note that in 861–62, a Viking fleet on the Seine divided into different groups based on the *sodalidates* (brotherhoods) that made up the fleet. These brotherhoods may have been small, such as a single ship's crew, or much larger, such as a fleet of several longships (Williams 2019: 18). While operating independently, Viking brotherhoods or fellowships could combine with other independent forces to achieve a common goal, such as occupying Frankish territory along the Seine. This informal method of organization appeared in England in 865 when the Anglo-Saxons fought against the Great Heathen Army, a coalition of warriors that originated from across Scandinavia.

Whether as members of a *hirð* or a *félag*, Viking warriors needed to identify one another on the battlefield, something that was probably achieved through physical appearance (Williams 2019: 29). Eyewitness Arabic accounts describe

Replica 10th-century Viking conical helmets. Pictorial sources indicate that a conical helmet with a nasal guard was the most common form of Scandinavian headgear, at least towards the end of the Viking Age. Examples are known from northern and eastern Europe. Conical helmets would have been made of boiled leather or metal plates, the leather variants being lighter and cooler to wear while still providing some protection against hostile blows (Williams 2019: 25). (DEA/C. BALOSSINI/Getty Images)

Viking men as wearing tattoos, and a shared design would likely have been worn among warriors of the same military group. An interesting custom of engraving one's teeth with horizontal file marks may have identified particular warbands. Common identity among warriors may have also been expressed through weapons and armour. It has been suggested that a collection of distinctively shaped Viking shield bosses from France and another from Ireland represented a particular group of Scandinavians that used them. Likewise, a bird design found on scabbard mounts from the Viking garrison at Birka in Sweden may have been a symbol that identified that group of warriors, or a much larger group of warriors, as that symbol has been found elsewhere in eastern Europe (Williams 2019: 29).

When considering these two categories of Viking warriors mentioned in historical sources, it is important to note that an individual might find himself in one or both groups at different times (Williams 2019: 28). Viking Age Scandinavia can accurately be described as a militarized society. In Scandinavia, all free men could, and probably did, carry weapons; and most free men would have had a familiarity with weapons, even if they were not warriors. This is because of the overlap between weapons of war that doubled as tools such as the spear, often used for hunting, the axe and the knife. Free men would have also wished to defend their families against warring factions of other Scandinavians. Indeed, Viking raids were not limited to foreign shores and occurred in Scandinavia just as in other parts of the world.

Within Scandinavian society, any free man who wished to pursue a career as a warrior was – if possessing the ability and given the opportunity – able to do so (Williams 2019: 27). In this regard, men who came from warrior families or wealthy backgrounds likely had more opportunities to seek a warrior's career. This was due to the cost of weapons and armour and the necessary training that might prove lifesaving in the heat of battle. Old Norse sagas suggest that it was relatively common for a young man of good standing to spend his early life raiding and warring, gaining wealth, social status and a reputation, before settling down to a more peaceful life as a farmer or landowner. *Orkneyinga saga*, a medieval history of the Orkney and Shetland islands, describes the life of a Viking chieftain named Svein Asleifarson. He appears throughout this saga as a warrior in the service of various earls and participates in raids against neighbouring chieftains and traders outside the realm of Orkney. Svein maintained a large following of his own warriors through the distribution of plunder; this enabled him to lead many successful ventures. The saga explains Svein's annual routine and, although depicting events of the mid-12th century, allows one to assume that chieftains of the Viking Age partook in a similar lifestyle. As related in the saga, Svein's annual routine consisted of planting the crops, departing on a spring raiding expedition, returning home to harvest the crops, departing on an autumn raiding expedition and then remaining at home during the winter before repeating the cycle the following year (Williams 2019: 37).

Frankish

If a Viking raiding party overcame resistance offered by the coast guard, the Frankish king might dispatch the royal host to oppose them. This occurred in 845 at the behest of Charles the Bald and again in 852, when Charles and his brother Lothair I (795–855) laid siege to the Viking camp at Jeufosse (Coupland 2004: 54). But how was the royal host summoned and directed?

In the last decade of the 8th century, around the time of the first Viking attack on Noirmoutier, the mobilization of Frankish troops is believed to have occurred in two stages (Ganshof 1970: 62–63). First, the military authorities received an order to alert those required to take up arms and ensure that those men already owing service were prepared to set out with their equipment and face the enemy in battle. Second, the order to assemble triggered these forces' movement to an agreed assembly point.

The mobilization of the host could be a slow process. The lapse of time between the alert of an encroaching enemy and the assembly of Frankish defenders depended upon circumstances, but could take several months. To address this problem, the Franks succeeded in organizing another defensive force to counter the Vikings on land. During the reign of Charlemagne, all subjects of the king, even subjugated peoples such as the Saxons, owed him military service. This service was required in the case of an enemy invasion and only applied in the region where such an attack occurred. The general Frankish call to arms in the face of an enemy invasion involved the men of the *lantweri*, a force made up of adult males from across the entire Frankish population, even including those who were normally forbidden to bear weapons. Coupland has noted that the motivation of those men of the *lantweri* who were mustered to defend their own homes – rather than the distant lands of their king, or territories beyond the boundaries of Francia – would have been high, perhaps even surpassing that of the royal host (Coupland 2004: 53).

This 9th-century fresco depicts a Frankish warlord who might represent Charlemagne, bearing a sword. In 781, Charlemagne is known to have forbidden the export of Frankish arms, while his grandson, Charles the Bald, made reference to the provision of weapons to the Vikings in the Edict of Pîtres (25 June 864). (De Agostini/ Getty Images)

This gold *solidus* shows the Byzantine emperor Leo VI (866–912; r. 886–912), known as 'the Wise'. While the Frankish cavalry were highly mobile shock troops who gained a formidable reputation in combat, they were not universally admired. A military treatise written in the late 9th or early 10th century and attributed to Leo VI stated that the Frankish cavalry lacked tactical sophistication and neglected proper reconnaissance (Nicolle 2005: 50). Evidence suggests that Frankish cavalrymen favoured sudden charges and operated as swift shock troops intent on breaking enemy formations. This notion is supported by Leo VI, who asserted that the Frankish cavalry struggled in difficult terrain and were particularly vulnerable to ambushes against the flanks or rear of their formations; a feigned flight on the enemy's part would prompt the Frankish cavalry to break ranks and mount a pursuit, leaving themselves vulnerable to counter-attack (Nicolle 2005: 50). Frankish cavalry could also operate on foot, as they did at Louvain in 891 (see page 67). (Fine Art Images/Heritage Images/Getty Images)

As Charlemagne's reign gave way to that of Louis the Pious, the Franks sought to accelerate the speed of mobilization (Ganshof 1970: 63–64). Chains of communication were established, in which an alert of an attack was received by each bishop who would, in turn, relay this to his own men and also transmit the information to counts, abbots and other local leaders. Upon receiving the alert order, those who served had to keep themselves ready and equipped to begin marching within 12 hours, thereby improving their reaction time once the assembly point had been established.

All men owning property were theoretically required to provide military service, with the wealthiest obliged to serve in person; less wealthy property-owners combined their resources, forming small groups in which one man went to war with the financial help of one, two, three or four others (Coupland 2004: 54). Those who owned a horse were required to bring their steed as well. Impoverished free men were exempt. The men of the *lantweri* were probably not well equipped when compared to the royal host, as most commoners could not afford anything more than a spear or bow. The roles of the coast guard were primarily assigned to the Frankish aristocracy, but everyone living along the coastline was required to support the regular guards in the case of an attack. Free men who failed to show support during an assault were fined 20 *solidi* (for comparison, a peasant's cow was worth three), and unfree men were fined ten *solidi* and received a flogging. In practice, however, it is likely that both the Frankish military leadership and the wider population preferred to leave the business of fighting to the warrior elite, with the bulk of the Frankish population continuing to work the land and support the military effort through their taxes (Nicolle 2005: 9).

While it is clear that cavalry formed a substantial part of Frankish armies during the Viking Age, it is not clear whether the majority of Carolingian warriors went to war on horseback. Frankish horsemen could fight on foot if required to by tactical circumstances, even if they were unused to doing so, as Coupland notes of the battle of Louvain in 891 (Coupland 2004: 61–62).

During the Viking Age, Frankish infantrymen were each equipped with a spear and shield; some sources state that infantrymen were also required to bring bows and arrows with them on campaign (Coupland 1990). According to surviving documents of the late 8th century, the well-heeled Frankish cavalryman's arms consisted of a spear and shield, a *spata* (long sword) and a *semispatum* (short sword), another term used for the single-edged dagger (Ganshof 1970: 65). Some Frankish cavalry were well-armoured; these horsemen wore a *brunia* (body armour), with some adding a *galea* (metal helmet) and *bauga* (metal arm-guards) and/or *bagnbergas* (leg armour). Armour worn by cavalrymen was immensely expensive. The mount and complete equipment of the Frankish horseman at the time of Charlemagne was equal to the value of 18–20 cows (Ganshof 1970: 66).

Some particularly well-trained and -equipped troops were earmarked for 'special operations' distinct from those carried out by the main field army; these operations ranged from raiding and reconnaissance to the garrisoning of important fortifications (Ganshof 1970: 64). It seems likely that the monarch would have been escorted by such a contingent.

CONDUCT IN BATTLE

While pitched battles and sieges were relatively rare, the two sides often came to blows in smaller, more fluid engagements. Vikings and Franks wielded broadly similar weapons, but their battle tactics appear to have been rather different; their very divergent objectives and the presence or absence of available reinforcements must have informed their approach to combat.

Viking

Vikings fought in groups of individual warriors rather than formal armies for most of the Viking Age. The weapons a warrior carried depended on his own means and the wealth of his chieftain, who might provide arms in exchange for his warriors' service and loyalty.

Although there are few detailed accounts of Viking Age battles, those that do exist imply that it was normal to fight in close formation (Williams 2019: 42). Contemporary stone and carving illustrations depict ranks of men with overlapping shields, suggesting the usage of shield-wall defensive tactics. These tactics seem to have been used by contemporaries of the Vikings, namely the Anglo-Saxons. The Viking shield-wall was composed of one or more rows of men overlapping their shields while thrusting their weapons through the angles of overlap within the wall formation. If a shield-wall consisted of multiple ranks, spearmen in the rear ranks could thrust through the gaps between the warriors in front of them. This, of course, strengthened the defence of the line and would prove to be deadly for charging Frankish cavalry units.

Another close formation referenced in literary sources has come to be known as the 'boar-snout' (Williams 2019: 47). This formation involved creating a wedge-shaped version of the shield-wall, with one or two warriors at the front forming the 'snout', and the other men forming shield-walls on either side of them angling backwards. This wedge-shaped formation would have been filled with additional angled ranks, bearing their shields to support the rank directly in front of them. The shields would then be tightly locked together, as the primary weapon was the shield-wall itself, supplemented by whatever other weapons the warriors were wielding. The boar-snout served as a human battering-ram used to puncture an opposing formation. Once formed, the shield-wall would charge an opposing formation at great speed, hoping to break through the enemy line. To be effective, the boar-snout required the men involved to be disciplined, moving at the same speed and not breaking ranks. The shield-wall and boar-snout are the only Scandinavian battlefield tactics recorded from the Viking Age; one may assume, however, that the Vikings employed others also.

Loose-formation tactics were most likely employed by the Vikings for the majority of their small raids. Indeed, their targets were sought out because of the minimal resistance they offered. For this reason, small raids could be carried out by a limited number of warriors, making battlefield tactics unnecessary and difficult to employ. In many cases, the successes of loose-formation tactics came down to the individual warrior's combat skill.

Dating from the 9th or 10th centuries, this German or West Slavic iron stirrup was found in northern Poland. Horses were well understood at the time to be central to the Frankish effort to counter the Viking threat, offering tactical mobility as well as enhanced combat effectiveness; the Edict of Pîtres stated that all warriors who owned horses were required to bring them on campaign (Coupland 2004: 63). Horses were also an important military asset for many of the cultures neighbouring the Franks. Equine diseases could severely degrade the effectiveness of the forces available to the Frankish crown, however; one such outbreak, in 791, killed fully 10 per cent of the Franks' horses (Nelson 2020: 326). While the Frankish stud-farms could make good this loss within three years, Charlemagne's Avar opponents were even more badly affected, lacking as they did the Franks' resilience. (Sepia Times/Universal Images Group via Getty Images)

These Viking spearheads, dated to the 10th century, were recovered from the Telemark and Hedmark regions in Norway. The spear was one of the most common weapons available to Scandinavians; but while affordable to many, they were not necessarily low-status weapons as some surviving examples feature pattern-welded blades and inlaid silver wire. Spears were used for both thrusting and throwing, this being reflected in the variety of sizes and shapes of Scandinavian spearheads. Some excavated graves contained multiple spears, suggesting that a warrior may have begun the battle by throwing lighter spears then reverted to thrusting once these weapons had been thrown (Williams 2019: 10). (PHAS/Universal Images Group via Getty Images)

It should be noted that missile combat played an important role during the Viking Age. While there is much debate as to whether the typical Viking warrior was also an archer, it is certain that the Vikings employed archery in battle in addition to throwing spears and smaller axes, which survive within the archaeological record; arrowheads embedded in the late-10th-century fortresses at Trelleborg in Denmark confirm the use of archery in combat (Williams 2019: 22). It is possible that Viking archers were generally lightly armed auxiliaries rather than the typical infantrymen who fought at close quarters in battle. A complete Scandinavian bow dating from the Viking Age – a longbow made of yew – was found in the Danish *emporium* (trading centre) of Hedeby. Experimentation with replicas of this longbow indicate that it had a draw-weight of up to 104lb and a range of up to 180m (Williams 2019: 23). Most arrowheads were leaf-shaped, suitable for hunting or use against an unarmoured foe, while bodkin-type arrowheads were used by the Vikings in battle.

Where surviving sources refer to ranged combat, it is often referenced in the context of a 'storm' of missiles. This 'storm' was likely to occur at the beginning of a battle, but was not limited to that timeframe (Williams 2019: 10). The use of missile weapons may have also been used as a tactic specifically to target enemy leaders as there are numerous accounts of leaders being wounded or killed by arrows or throwing spears. In any case, a leader's death in battle was often a decisive event, and it seems that long-range missile tactics could be employed to meet this end.

Accompanied here by shield bosses from Telemark (left; 10th century) and Hedmark (right; 11th century), this 10th-century axe-head was found in Oppland, Norway. Much like the spear, the axe was affordable and easy to produce in its simplest form. It was not necessarily a low-status weapon as numerous surviving axe-heads are ornamented with silver and gold (Williams 2019: 10). Axes were crafted in a variety of shapes and sizes, often doubling as tools. Larger axes were used on a double-handed shaft that might be long enough to reach the wielder's shoulder. These types of axes, with broad curved blades, were particularly common in Denmark and seem to have been an innovation of the 10th century (Williams 2019: 12). (PHAS/Universal Images Group via Getty Images)

Made from silver, this 'Thor's Hammer' amulet dates from the 9th century. While Vikings were sustained by their traditional beliefs, sometimes forswearing them in favour of Christianity and at other times appearing to hedge their bets, the Franks believed in a God of immense power, capable of directing the outcome of their many battles against the Vikings. (CM Dixon/Print Collector/Getty Images)

Siege warfare was employed by the Vikings in Francia on multiple occasions, most notably during the siege of Paris in 885–86. In the siege, the Frankish *Annals of Saint-Vaast* mention the use of a battering-ram and of *machinae*, which might imply a variety of siege weapons. With regard to siege tactics, the Vikings seem to have favoured the use of fire and archery, as the archaeological remains of the Danish fortress at Trelleborg suggest. A siege attempt employed by the Vikings at Chester in 907 involved their use of wicker hurdles covered in hides and supported with posts to protect themselves against hot liquids and missile attacks as they tried to undermine the city walls (Williams 2019: 56). While there is no direct evidence for the use of Scandinavian siege equipment apart from battering-rams, it is possible that the Vikings gained familiarity with *ballistae* (forms of catapults) just as they had with other types of Frankish weaponry.

Frankish

Like other armies of the era, the Franks deployed scouts in order to ascertain enemy intentions and gather information. For example, the West Frankish king Louis III (863–82; r. 879–82) defeated a group of Vikings at Saucourt-en-Vimeu on 3 August 881 after he employed scouts, who spotted the Northmen returning from a successful raid carrying the fruits of their attack (Coupland 2004: 67). The Franks also worked to trick the raiders: in 873 Charles the Bald misdirected the Viking contingent at Angers by advertising his intention to take his army into Brittany rather than attacking Angers.

Coupland concludes (2004: 68) that the Frankish forces meeting the Vikings in pitched battle would have favoured the close-order battle tactics

Foot soldiers of the 10th century are shown in this detail from the Echternach Gospels, depicting the parable of the vineyard. The shields depicted in this illustration are of a distinctive, almond-shaped 'kite' style. The portrayal of 10th-century Franks using this type of shield could have been influenced by foreign artistic traditions. In regions where Frankish authority was weak, men of the *lantweri* might organize themselves independently, as occurred in 867 when the Danish chieftain Rorik was driven out of Frisia (Nelson 1991: 139–40). The local initiatives of the *lantweri* were carried out with varying degrees of success against the Vikings. In 869, two counts, Hugh and Gauzfrid, led men of the *Transsequanani* (those residing between the Seine and the Loire) to victory over a group of Scandinavians operating in the Loire Valley (Coupland 2004: 53–54). Conversely, Regino of Prüm chronicles a defeat suffered in 882 by the *lantweri* of his region at the hands of the Northmen, claiming that the undisciplined Frankish combatants were slaughtered by their Danish opponents. (Bildagentur-online/Universal Images Group via Getty Images)

they used against other opponents. Seasoned Frankish troops could employ a variety of approaches to maximize their chances of success in combat, from the use of poor light to the setting of ambushes; for obvious reasons, the tactical options available to less effective Frankish troops were much more limited. The Franks were used to fighting open-order opponents such as the Bretons, who fought in dispersed order and feigned retreat to tempt the Frankish troops into mounting an impetuous pursuit.

The battlefield role of Frankish infantry is unclear. British historian David Nicolle notes that the apparent reappearance of massed infantry tactics in the period immediately preceding the Viking Age may simply be a result of most warfare of that era taking place in eastern portions of the Frankish Empire, where the availability of horses was restricted (Nicolle 1984: 8). Carolingian infantrymen, such as those whom Charles Martel commanded in 732 at the battle of Poitiers (Bachrach 2001: 95), were expected to achieve more than simply holding the line while in combat. Marching was critical to the mobility of Frankish troops, who sang songs and recited verses while on the move. When advancing, it was important that the Franks retained their formation and they were trained to do so at a slow walk over ancient Roman roads and rough terrain alike (Bachrach 2001: 98).

The Franks appear to have lacked the maritime technology necessary to implement successful amphibious operations against Viking encampments. Charles the Bald sent such an expedition against a group of Vikings camped on an island in the Seine in 852, but the plan failed as the Franks lacked the appropriate watercraft to transport their men to the island. Smaller boats were used by the Franks in military operations, but served as ferries rather than as jumping-off points for an attack, because the boats' draught meant they could not be landed on the beaches of an occupied island.

The First Clashes

799–840

BACKGROUND TO BATTLE

It was during the Saxon Wars (772–804) that the Danes first came to the Frankish king's attention. As Charlemagne waged a savage campaign of conquest in Saxony, the chronicles of the Carolingian court made reference to 'Nordmannia' (Denmark). In 777, the Frankish king held an assembly that the Saxon leader Widukind did not attend, as he had reportedly fled into this mysterious region (Scholz 1970: 55). In 782, envoys of the Danish king, Sigfrid, arrived at Charlemagne's court: Widukind's reappearance in Saxony soon afterwards may have resulted from this encounter (Nelson 1997: 20). Widukind would go on to lead the Saxon resistance to Frankish rule and the imposition of Christianity until he agreed to surrender in 785, but various groups of Saxons would intermittently continue to resist Frankish overlordship for nearly 20 more years.

A silver *denarius* of Charlemagne. It is believed that coins bearing Charlemagne's imperial title were minted only after 812, when he received recognition as emperor of the West. Note the 'M' on this coin standing for Mainz, indicating where it was made. (Christophel Fine Art/Universal Images Group via Getty Images)

As the Saxon Wars came to a close, Charlemagne worked to defend his realm against external threats. In March 800, the Frankish king left his palace in Aachen, heading for the Channel to oversee the construction of coastal defences. On Christmas Day 800, Charlemagne was crowned as Emperor of the Romans by Pope Leo III. In 804, the emperor's forces crushed one final Saxon rebellion, marking the end of the conflict. This campaign sparked the interest of the Danish king Godfred (r. *c.*804–10) who, according to the *Royal Frankish Annals*, brought his fleet and army to the Saxon–Danish border that year; he agreed to meet Charlemagne, but was persuaded by his followers not to do so, and kept his distance (Scholz 1970: 83). These annals go on to relate that Godfred subsequently overcame his wariness, and the Danes embarked on a campaign of piracy, sending ships to harry the shores of the Frankish Empire.

A replica 10th-century Viking shield. With regard to archaeological finds, metal bosses are generally the only piece of a shield that survive; 32 complete shields have, however, been found in the Gokstad ship burial at Vestfold, Norway, and wooden fragments of a shield were found at Trelleborg, Denmark, as well. Leather rims sewn around the edge of the shield (as shown here) appear to have been more common than similar metal rims. Viking shields were likely painted in an array of different colours and often displayed decorative artwork. Of the shields found in the Gokstad ship, half are painted in black and half in yellow. (DEA/C. BALOSSINI/ Getty Images)

OPPOSITE

This illustration from the *Annals of Fulda* depicts Charlemagne (left) with his eldest son Pepin (*c.*768–811), known as 'the Hunchback', who was disgraced and exiled to the monastery of Prüm after his 792 revolt. Like his brother Charles the Younger (*c.*772–811), Pepin predeceased his father, effectively removing a potential problem for Charlemagne's heir, Louis the Pious. (API/Gamma-Rapho via Getty Images)

A dragon-prowed Viking longship featured in a 10th-century Anglo-Saxon manuscript. Commonly depicted with shields lining either side of the wooden vessels, longships could also provide a platform from which Viking archers could use missile weapons against their enemies while being protected by a boundary of water themselves. Without the versatility of the longships, Scandinavian military success in Francia would have likely been impossible. (Ann Ronan Pictures/Print Collector/ Getty Images)

In 802, 806 and 810, the Franks made further preparations to defend the waterways that led into the heartland of their empire. Warriors were stationed at the mouths of the empire's major rivers – notably, the Meuse, Seine and Loire – and defensive fortifications were constructed at these points. The Frankish effort to defend the coast continued as the empire passed from Charlemagne to his son Louis the Pious in 814. In 834, however, Dorestad, a vital Frankish trading centre located in Frisia, fell prey to Scandinavian raiders. Frisia, which encompassed the land stretched along the North Sea from Denmark to the Netherlands, was difficult to defend without a proper fleet, something the Franks had always lacked. The fact that Scandinavians could penetrate Frankish defences as far inland as Dorestad demonstrated Louis the Pious's inability to maintain his father's coastal-defence system. This military failure would prove fateful for the Franks in the years that followed Louis's death in 840.

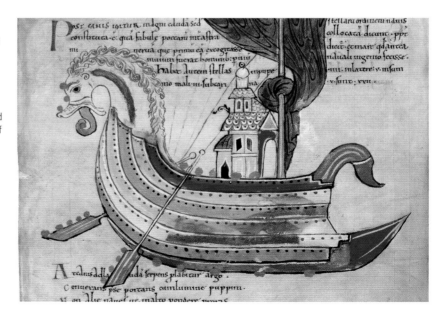

1 799: The first Viking raid in Francia is recorded. A warband of Northmen plunder the island of Noirmoutier, a hub for the salt and wine trades and home to the monastery of Saint-Philibert. A contingent of Frankish warriors meet the Vikings in battle. Over 100 of the Northmen are killed, and some of their longships are destroyed.

2 808: At the behest of King Godfred, the Danes improve the fortifications known as the Danevirke, in a bid to deter the Franks from invading Danish territory.

3 808: Danish forces destroy Reric, an Obotrite trading post that competed with Danish Hedeby.

4 810: A Viking fleet of 200 ships sails from Denmark and ravages all the islands along the Frisian coast. The Frankish royal host is dispatched and three battles are fought, but the Northmen are victorious, extracting 100lb of silver as tribute.

5 810: Charlemagne and the Frankish royal host await Godfred's field army near the River Weser, but the Danish king is killed by one of his own men before the two sides meet.

6 811: Godfred's successor, his nephew Hemming, seeks peace with the Franks; initially delayed by poor winter weather, Danish envoys travel to Aachen to agree the Treaty of Heiligen, which establishes the Danish border at the River Eider.

7 811: Charlemagne orders the construction of a fleet and inspects newly built ships at Boulogne and Ghent.

8 812–14: Denmark is riven by civil war in the wake of Hemming's death.

9 815: Exiled from Denmark in 814, former Danish king Harald 'Klak' Halfdansson enlists the help of the new Frankish emperor, Louis the Pious; Harald takes a Saxon/Obotrite army into Denmark, but the Danes refuse battle and the raiders return to Francia. A second expedition, this time successful, follows in 819.

10 820: A fleet of 13 Viking ships attempts to raid the Flemish coast, but is repulsed; a second raid at the mouth of the River Seine is also rebuffed, and the raiders target Bouin in Aquitaine instead.

11 826: Harald Klak is baptized and given the county of Rüstringen in Frisia as a base; although Harald is deposed as king for a second time in 827, this award of territory ushers in a 70-year period during which Frisia is held by various Viking leaders with Carolingian approval.

12 831: Following a period of Frankish civil war, Louis the Pious is reinstated as emperor at Nijmegen; his son Lothair is pardoned but disgraced.

13 834: A large Viking fleet penetrates 80km into the Rhine delta and sacks the Frisian trading centre of Dorestad. The Vikings return to Dorestad in 835, 836 and 837.

14 836: At the Diet of Crémieu, Louis the Pious attempts to restore good faith after a second period of Frankish civil war involving the emperor and his sons Pepin, Louis the German and Lothair.

15 20 June 840: Exhausted by a third bout of civil war among the Frankish elite, Louis the Pious dies at Ingolstadt. The Frankish Empire is plunged into internecine strife once more.

Battlefield environment

After their initial raid on Noirmoutier in 799, the Vikings would occupy the island time and again during ensuing years. As the focus of Scandinavian activity shifted, however, the Viking base on Noirmoutier seems to have been abandoned. In 819, the abbot of Saint-Philibert, Arnulf, noted that his order suffered attacks from Northmen who frequently ravaged the monastery (Adrien 2018). The Northmen established a base on Noirmoutier to store plunder from their attacks on the nearby city of Nantes. From this base, the Vikings launched regular raids into Brittany and along the River Loire. In places such as Frisia, the Frankish coast was challenging to defend. This coastal region, criss-crossed by navigable rivers and estuaries, provided the Vikings with many potential areas in which they could launch raiding parties from their longships. Without a good fleet, the Frankish coast guard found that a proper defence of Frisia was a hopeless task.

Owing to the network of waterways that criss-crossed Frisia, Dorestad was easily accessible to Viking marauders in the 830s. The fact that Dorestad was a major *emporium* (trading centre) during the Viking Age suggests that the Scandinavians were well aware of its riches before they first raided the town. The town itself is known to have stretched along the bank of the River Rhine. If the Frankish defenders were alerted to the Viking presence, one could imagine that they used Dorestad's townscape to their defensive advantage. Houses and warehouses of wood and thatch would have provided suitable (though flammable) makeshift fortifications in the event of a Viking assault. The fortified enclosure outside of Dorestad may also have provided the townspeople with protection during a Viking attack. Protected by a ditch and bank, it appears to have been constructed with minimal resources.

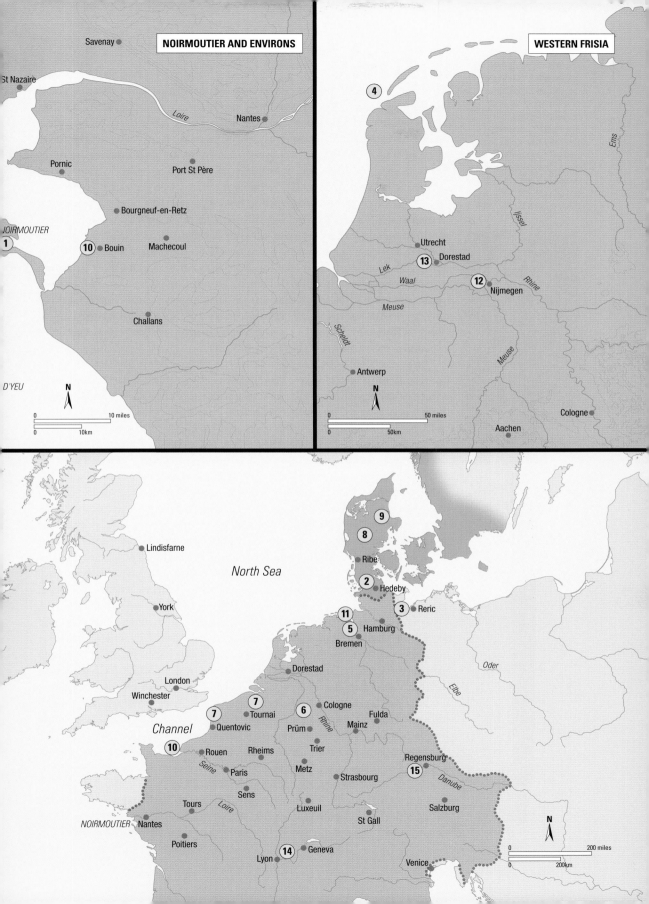

NOIRMOUTIER AND ENVIRONS

Savenay

St Nazaire

Loire

Nantes

Pornic

Port St Père

Bourgneuf-en-Retz

JOIRMOUTIER

① ⑩ Bouin

Machecoul

Challans

D'YEU

N

0 — 10 miles
0 — 10km

WESTERN FRISIA

④

Ems

IJssel

Utrecht

⑬ Dorestad

Lek

Waal

⑫ Nijmegen

Rhine

Meuse

Scheldt

Meuse

Antwerp

Cologne

N

Aachen

0 — 50 miles
0 — 50km

Lindisfarne

North Sea

⑨

⑧

Ribe

York

② Hedeby

③ Reric

⑪

⑤ Hamburg

Bremen

Oder

London

Dorestad

Elbe

Winchester

⑦ ⑦ Tournai

⑥ Cologne

Channel

Quentovic

Fulda

Prüm

Mainz

Rhine

⑩ Rouen

Rheims

Trier

Regensburg

Seine

Paris

Metz

⑮

Danube

Sens

Strasbourg

NOIRMOUTIER Nantes

Tours

Loire

Luxeuil

Salzburg

Poitiers

St Gall

⑭ Geneva

Lyon

Venice

N

0 — 200 miles
0 — 200km

INTO COMBAT

Although the initial Viking raid in 799 had occurred on the Atlantic coast, the primary focus of Viking activity within Francia was in the North Sea. The Danish monarchy appears to have played a much more overt role in these early raids than it did subsequently, with the relationship between the rulers of Francia and Denmark, having so recently become neighbours owing to Frankish military expansion, informing the Vikings' activities.

The attacks on Frisia in 810 are known to have been politically motivated. In 808, Godfred had ordered work to be carried out on a border fortification known as the Danevirke, seeking to protect Denmark from Frankish invasion. Godfred attacked the Obotrites, allies of the Franks, and made an alliance with the Wilzes, a neighbouring Slavic people hostile to the Obotrites (Nelson 1997: 21). Godfred also ordered the destruction of Reric, an Obotrite trading post that offered competition to Hedeby, prompting its traders to move their operations to that Danish settlement. In 809, negotiations between Godfred and the Franks collapsed; a Frankish fortress was constructed on the Danish border (Roesdahl 2016: 141), and Charlemagne was planning a military expedition into Denmark (Nelson 1997: 21).

After the Danes became aware of the construction of Charlemagne's fortress, Godfred decided to make his own show of force by attacking Frisia, a vast coastal expanse that had, for many years, been the focus of Scandinavian ambitions. Stretching along the North Sea coast from Denmark to the modern-day Netherlands, Frisia was nearly impossible to defend without a proper fleet, which the Franks did not have. The size of the invading Viking fleet is reported as 200 ships. While this number was likely inflated by Frankish chroniclers for dramatic effect, there is no reason not to believe that Godfred sent a fleet of considerable size. This fleet ravaged all the islands along the Frisian coast and fought three battles in the region, according to the *Royal Frankish Annals*. Commercial trading centres appear to have been the favoured targets of the Viking attackers. This was probably due to the obvious allure of portable wealth (i.e. trade goods) and the region's comparative lack of vulnerable monasteries. The Frankish royal host was subsequently dispatched, but the Northmen were victorious, extracting 100lb of silver from Frisia as tribute.

Following the initial attacks of 810, Charlemagne mobilized his forces and waited for Godfred by the River Weser. The *Royal Frankish Annals* relate that Godfred was inflated by the vain hope of victory, for he had boasted that he wished to fight the Frankish king in open battle; but it was reported to Charlemagne that the Viking fleet that had ravaged Frisia had returned to Denmark, and that Godfred had been slain by one of his own men. After the death of Godfred, his nephew Hemming succeeded to the Danish throne (r. 810–12) and swiftly sought peace with the Franks, but poor winter weather hampered travel for the swearing of oaths to seal the agreement (Scholz 1970: 93). In 811, Danish envoys did travel to Aachen to meet Charlemagne and agreed the Treaty of Heiligen, which established the Danish border at the River Eider.

In response to the Viking attacks on Frisia, Charlemagne ordered the construction of a fleet and inspected the newly built ships at Boulogne and Ghent in 811 (Coupland 2004: 50). After the initial Scandinavian attack on

Frisia, there was an overall increase in Frankish security measures, principally involving guard service and maintaining a state of alert. In addition, ships were assembled or constructed so as to create flotillas that were deployed on navigable waterways.

Nelson points out (1997: 21–22) that Hemming was a capable and effective early-medieval ruler, being able to direct major building projects, summon and deploy fleets, and understand the importance of trade and tolls. In 812, dynastic disputes erupted among the Danes as news spread that Hemming had died, focusing Danish political attention inwards and away from relations with their Frankish neighbours. A Dane called Harald 'Klak' Halfdansson (*c*.785–*c*.852) emerged as a new king in Denmark, but he was forced into exile and fled to Francia. In the years following 810, however, Viking raiding activity in Frisia had continued. After several centuries of mostly peaceful interactions between the Northmen and Franks, Scandinavian seafarers would have been well-informed as to the whereabouts and vulnerabilities of their potential targets. Peripheral communities seem to have been mostly unprepared and undefended, easily approachable by sea but difficult to reach and protect with land forces such as the Frankish royal host.

In characteristic Viking fashion, the acquisition of portable wealth seems to have been the primary goal of these excursions. References to the plunder of such wealth are ample. Whether religious or commercial in origin, the spoils of Viking raids were vast, ranging from precious metals to foodstuffs. As occurred in 810, the Northmen exacted tribute payments from their often-defenceless victims. Instances of Viking captive-taking are also known to have occurred. Along with the earlier capture of the Frankish deacon, Aldulf, in 809, Scandinavian assailants were reported to have carried off an unknown number of prisoners in 813 and 834 (Cooijmans 2020: 203).

A reconstruction of a Frankish village typical of the southern areas of the Carolingian Empire during the 9th and 10th centuries. In Dorestad, far to the north, similar buildings made of wood, clay and thatch would have provided the Frankish defenders with only limited protection against the Vikings in 834 and subsequently. During the 9th century, Frankish villages were frequently looted and burned by Viking and other raiders in search of provisions. (Parco Archeologico di Poggibonsi/ Camillo Balossini/Mondadori Portfolio via Getty Images)

A bronze Viking spearhead, its socket lavishly decorated with silver. The majority of the archaeological evidence for Scandinavian spears during the Viking Age has been found in graves, although some materials have been retrieved from bogs and rivers (Williams 2019: 9). Because of the varying conditions, it is normally only the spearheads that survive, their wooden shafts having perished due to the elements of weather and time. In addition to being a weapon of the common warrior, spears bearing heads such as this were also used by the Scandinavian elite. (Werner Forman/Universal Images Group/Getty Images)

On 28 January 814, Charlemagne died, having crowned his only surviving son, Louis the Pious, as co-emperor on 11 September 813, thereby nominating him as his successor. The sheer length of Charlemagne's reign – 768–814 – and the harsh realities of life expectancy in the early medieval period meant that all bar one of his sons predeceased him. This perpetuated the unusual situation whereby the Frankish lands remained a single polity, as the legal requirement for Charlemagne to provide for all of his male heirs, thereby dividing the Frankish realm, did not apply. Louis was determined to preserve the unity of the Frankish Empire, so in an unfortunately precipitate move, in 817 he issued an imperial decree known as the *Ordinatio imperii*, setting out his succession plans for each of his three sons: Lothair (795–855), Pepin (797–838) and Louis (*c.*806–76).

While Louis's plan immediately fostered rivalry and resentment among the three brothers, it was his marriage to Judith of Bavaria in 819 and the subsequent birth of her son Charles (823–77), later called 'the Bald', that really endangered Louis's plans for the Frankish Empire. Louis's wish to provide for his fourth son angered his three older heirs, starting in 829, when Alemannia, formerly part of Lothair's inheritance, was given to Charles. Lothair accused Judith of adultery, thereby questioning Charles's legitimacy, and raised an army in revolt; a major confrontation ensued in 830–31, after which Lothair was pardoned but disgraced.

Despite Louis's attempts to restore order, a second rebellion followed in 832, this time with Pepin at its heart. Louis decided to adjust his succession plans once again, the result being that all parties remained discontented; in the ensuing machinations Louis was humiliated and effectively deposed, and even after he was restored as emperor in March 834 his imperial authority was seriously undermined. In 836 a family reconciliation of sorts occurred, but the message to the Franks' neighbours and subject peoples was clear: there was disunity at the heart of Louis's empire and ample opportunities for profit, plunder and even conquest at Frankish expense. A further revision of the succession followed in 837, with Charles the Bald favoured over his half-brothers; a third civil war ensued, with yet another succession settlement announced on 20 May 839.

At the beginning of Louis the Pious's reign in 814, the peoples on the frontiers of the Frankish Empire were quiescent. Soon, however, the Sorbs and then the Obotrites rebelled, joined by the Danes; the Slavs also threatened the area around Venice, and the Bulgarians recaptured territory formerly held by the Franks. Louis made efforts to neutralize the threat from the Franks' Danish neighbours, who were, according to the *Annals of Fulda*, the most important of the Nordic peoples on the Franks' northern frontier. The exile Harald Klak sought Louis's help in securing the throne of Denmark after his exile. In 815 Louis directed that the Saxons and Obotrites should aid Harald in his bid to regain the Danish throne, but although Harald's contingent crossed into Denmark and engaged in looting, the Danish army and fleet dared not engage them and the raiders returned to Francia.

Another attempt was made in 819, this time with more success; Harald appears to have been accepted by the Danes as a co-ruler alongside two of Godfred's sons. By 823, however, tensions between the co-rulers had reached such a pitch that Harald asked Louis to mediate. While some scholars see Louis's objective as the outright conquest of the Danes, others maintain that the Frankish emperor sought to draw Denmark into the Frankish orbit as a protectorate (Coupland 2007: 89). Louis's subsequent approach to Harald would involve the usual elements of Frankish diplomacy, but then shift dramatically to an entirely new approach that would transform the prospects of Frankish Frisia for decades to come.

Louis's diplomats advised Harald to convert to Christianity, a move Louis hoped would help to bring Denmark within the Frankish sphere of influence should Harald regain the Danish throne. The Franks had been working to send missionaries into Scandinavia for many years, and Louis was determined to continue this effort to spread the word of God among the Danes and their northern neighbours. There was a well-established practice among the Franks of seeking to persuade the leading men among Francia's neighbours and clients to accept baptism and be brought within

the Christian fold, as a means of bringing such individuals within the Frankish orbit. Harald duly obliged in 826, with Louis standing as his godfather, and was accepted by the nobles of the Frankish royal court.

In a major departure, however, Louis also gave Harald the county of Rüstringen in Frisia as a base, should his new-found Christian piety result in his expulsion from Denmark once again. In 827, this is exactly what happened; it seems that Harald's baptism indicated to his fellow Danes that he was simply too close to the Frankish regime (Parker 2014: 47). The award of Rüstringen to Harald was the start of a 70-year period during which much – and at times, all – of Frisia was held by various Viking leaders with the overt approval of the Carolingians (Parker 2014: 47). Whether Harald ever managed to reclaim power in Denmark itself is uncertain, as he soon disappears from the record. The *Annals of Saint-Bertin* mention a particular 'Harald' who in 841 was given the island of Walcheren in the mouth of the River Scheldt by Lothair I (see page 72), but this second individual was almost certainly not Harald Klak (Nelson 1991: 51).

Louis the Pious would strive to maintain his father's defences across the vast Frankish Empire, but was ultimately unable to do so. In the early years of Louis's reign, however, the coastal defences established by Charlemagne remained effective. This was demonstrated in 820, when a fleet of 13 Viking ships attempted to raid the Flemish coast; after being repulsed the Northmen sailed on to the mouth of the Seine. Here the Danes were attacked by the coast guard again, losing five of their number in combat, and were compelled

St John is depicted in this miniature from the Gospel of Ebo (*c*.775–851), archbishop of Rheims and one of Louis the Pious's chief advisors, *c*.820. Frankish clergymen played a vital role in the Frankish realm's struggle against the Vikings. According to a capitulary of 865, in the event of an invasion, local bishops, abbots and abbesses were instructed to dispatch their contingents of troops, equipped for battle and led by standard-bearers (Coupland 2004: 53). Examples of clergymen responsible for maintaining a defence against the Vikings appear in contemporary sources. In 854, Frankish troops led by Burchard, bishop of Chartres, and Agius, bishop of Orléans, forestalled a Viking attack on Orléans (Coupland 2004: 59). (DEA/G. DAGLI ORTI/ Getty Images)

Just as Viking chieftains and kings were honoured through oral histories and lavish burial customs, the Franks commemorated the finest of their warriors through written histories and pictorial sources. Here, Louis the Pious is depicted in warlike costume as a *miles Christi* ('warrior of Christ') in this manuscript image from Hrabanus Maurus's *De Laudibus sanctae crucis* (In Praise of the Holy Cross). The cross-staff held by Louis symbolizes victory over visible and invisible enemies. In the halo encircling the king's head are the words 'You, Christ, crown Louis.' (DEA/G. DAGLI ORTI/Getty Images)

to sail on further, this time to Bouin in Aquitaine, in the search for a suitably ill-defended site to attack (Coupland 2004: 51). By the 830s, however, frequent and successful Viking raids in Frisia and Aquitaine highlighted the decreasing effectiveness of the Franks' coastal defences.

In 834, in the wake of the second civil war to engulf Louis's troubled empire, a substantial Viking fleet attacked and looted the trading centre of Dorestad, situated close to the present-day town of Wijk bij Duurstede in the Netherlands. Dorestad sat at the junction of two important trading routes connecting Frisia with the Rhineland, Scandinavia, England and Frankish Neustria. This major economic hub had been coveted by the Franks for years before they subdued the Frisians during the 8th century and were subsequently able to benefit from the extraction of tolls and harbour fees levied upon the traders operating in the town. In the early 9th century, Dorestad's population was in the region of 2,000 and it covered an area of about 3 square kilometres, with the town stretching more than 3km along the bank of the Rhine (Haywood 2016: 80). While the Carolingians

The Dorestad Brooch (*c.*800) at an exhibition commemorating the 1,200th anniversary of Charlemagne's death in Aachen, Germany. The brooch was found in the remains of a well, prompting speculation that it might have been deposited there for safekeeping in a time of uncertainty. While Dorestad was a vital trading hub, it also was a hive of manufacturing activity. Craftspeople of many kinds, from shipwrights to jewellers, operated there, and valuable raw materials and high-value items such as wine and manufactured goods all passed through the town. (Sascha Schuermann/ Getty Images)

actively encouraged traders to congregate in the settlement, in the years before 834 it seems that the evolving economic situation had prompted the royal authorities to cede some measure of control over the town to the diocese of Utrecht. Even so, Dorestad presented a tempting target to Viking raiders well aware of the town's wealth and vulnerability in a time of Frankish political disarray.

Dorestad seems to have lacked proper defences, leaving it unprepared and easily overwhelmed by the Danish raiders. The town may have originally developed from an earlier settlement around an old *castellum* (Roman encampment). Nevertheless, it is dubious whether the fort was still being used as a defensive structure after the 5th century (Cooijmans 2015: 33).

Dorestad appears to have had three sectors: the harbour, or lower town; the trading centre, or upper town; and an area of farmland further inland, that presumably fed the inhabitants and visitors. A road linked the lower and upper parts of the settlement. Excavations in the lower town in the 1960s and 1970s revealed the remains of wooden causeways that would have aided the movement of raw materials and manufactured goods, whether completed in the town itself or transported from elsewhere. While the area along the riverbank was divided into plots to provide each trader with access to the water, the jumble of wooden dwellings, workshops and storage buildings beyond would have developed over decades of increasing economic activity; there was no surrounding wall, meaning the settlement was vulnerable to attack overland as well as from the water.

The timing of the Viking attack on Dorestad in 834 was intentional. Following the second unsuccessful revolt against Louis the Pious in 832– 34, the Northmen took advantage of the ongoing political disarray that afflicted the Frankish realm. By attacking during a time of political division, the Vikings reduced the risk of encountering substantial resistance along

Dorestad, 834

This illustration depicts a local contingent of Frankish defenders seeking to eject the Viking raiders who have descended on the *emporium* (trading centre) known as Dorestad. Having pillaged much of the town – a haphazard collection of wooden houses, storehouses and workshops – the raiders are making their way along one of the causeways, bearing the spoils of their raid. These Vikings are well-armoured with mail tunics and the linen clothes beneath these. They bear standard Scandinavian shields and swords, which they may have purloined from one of the storehouses in Dorestad. The meagre Frankish detachment attempting to block the raiders from proceeding further down the causeway are outnumbered and intimidated. They are mostly unarmoured, wearing linen tunics and wielding weapons similar to those of the Northmen.

the rivers on which they travelled. Furthermore, it has been argued that the Scandinavian attacks on Frisia were actively encouraged by Lothair I, perhaps aiming to weaken his father Louis the Pious's regime by restricting the flow of trade between the North Sea and the Rhineland.

While the Frankish chroniclers emphasize the carnage and mayhem of the Viking raid on Dorestad, it is hard to establish quite how devastating the raid actually was (Haywood 2016: 81). It was clearly not in the Northmen's interest to raze the settlement to the ground, as that would have precluded their return for more plunder – and the Vikings did indeed return in the following three years. In fact, it seems possible that the raids actually stimulated economic activity in the town, raising the intriguing possibility that Dorestad's traders and merchants were benefiting from the fruits of Viking activity elsewhere in Francia and further afield (Haywood 2016: 81).

Like his father Charlemagne, Louis the Pious ordered the construction of ships in Frisia to prevent further Viking attacks in the years following 834. The Frankish king also ordered the construction of forts to protect the Frisian coast and the Rhine delta. One of these forts, on the island of Walcheren, was captured by the Vikings in 837 as they made their way back to Dorestad, preparing to sack the town once more. Frankish casualties were high, and a number of men were captured by the Northmen. Louis took this setback so seriously that he cancelled a planned trip to Rome. The Frisians were blamed by the Franks for ignoring their military duties and not opposing the Vikings. In 838, however, a fifth Scandinavian attack on Dorestad was prevented when the Viking fleet was destroyed by a storm before it reached the shoreline. In the event, this did not matter. By this time, Northmen were active along Francia's entire northern coastline. It seemed they were virtually unstoppable.

Louis's efforts to pacify his Danish neighbours and maintain the Frankish coastal-defence system ultimately proved ineffectual, largely because of the internal strife that divided his realm. When Louis died on 20 June 840, Frankish internal struggles boiled over once again, as Louis's three surviving sons fought a civil war among themselves. The Vikings would take full advantage of this opportunity as the Frankish Empire fragmented.

The Great Assault

840–77

BACKGROUND TO BATTLE

The death of Louis the Pious marked the beginning of a new phase in the struggle between the Vikings and their Frankish neighbours. The civil wars between Louis and his sons had resulted in the dilution of Frankish efforts

This illumination from *De Laudibus sanctae crucis* depicts the work's author, Hrabanus Maurus (left), accompanied by his teacher Alcuin of York (middle), dedicating his work to Odgar, archbishop of Mainz (right). In 838–39, Odgar supported Louis the Pious against his son Louis the German, and transferred his allegiance to Lothair I during the civil war that broke out after the death of Louis the Pious on 20 June 840. Odgar reportedly attempted to prevent a meeting between Louis the German and Charles the Bald in 842. Odgar died on 21 April 847 and was succeeded by Hrabanus Maurus, who was archbishop of Mainz until his death on 4 February 856. (Photo 12/Universal Images Group via Getty Images)

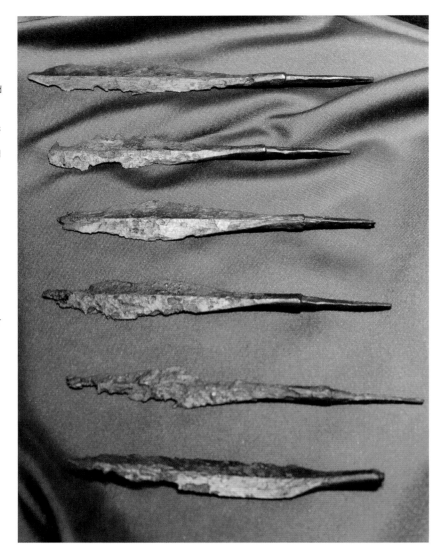

Six arrowheads recovered from a 9th-century grave in Norway. Norwegian law-codes dating from shortly after the Viking Age stated that a bow should be provided for every two warriors of the regional ship-levies serving the king. High-ranking leaders such as a chieftain at the battle of Svolder in 1000 used bows in battle, according to Old Norse sagas (Williams 2019: 22). Viking archers may have operated as lightly armoured auxiliaries as well as traditional warriors. This notion is suggested by the famous Bayeux Tapestry from the late Viking Age, which depicts unarmoured archers, and the fact that contemporary medieval cultures also employed archer auxiliaries (Williams 2019: 22). (PHAS/Universal Images Group via Getty Images)

to defend their coastline and river valleys. The opportunistic, small-scale Scandinavian raids of previous decades gave way to more ambitious, carefully planned attacks on Frankish centres of wealth and trade.

Following the announcement of Louis's death, on 24 July 840 his eldest son, Lothair, claimed overlordship over the entirety of the Frankish realm as it had been at the beginning of his father's reign, despite the machinations of the previous decades that had substantially redrawn Louis's succession plans for his descendants. This claim prompted Louis's other surviving sons, Louis the German and Charles the Bald, to form an alliance and move against their brother and his allies. The fateful battle of Fontenoy on 25 June 841 pitted the forces of Lothair I (r. 817–55) and his nephew Pepin II – son of Louis the Pious's second son Pepin, who had died in 838, and king of Aquitaine (r. 838–c.852) – against those of Louis the German and Charles the Bald. Lothair I's forces initially had the upper hand, but the arrival of reinforcements tipped the balance in favour of Louis the German and Charles the Bald.

In this miniature from the Vivian Bible (fol. 423), Count Vivian of Tours is surrounded by monks as he presents the Vivian Bible to Charles the Bald in 845. The oaths sworn at Strasbourg on 14 February 842 by Charles and his brother Louis the German were especially noteworthy as the wordings – Louis's oath in Old French, and Charles's oath in Old High German – have been preserved and offer important insights into the intricacies of these early European languages. Crucially, the two Frankish contingents swore to support and defend the two brothers not as their kings, or because they were French or German, but because of the bonds and obligations existing between a lord and his vassals. (DEA/J.E. BULLOZ/ Getty Images)

Lothair fled to Aachen, determined to continue the fight; on 14 February 842 his brothers responded by concluding the Oaths of Strasbourg, by which they affirmed their alliance by swearing a joint oath against Lothair and his imperial ambitions, in the presence of their respective armies. Lothair now realized that he would have to negotiate with his brothers and their allies, and in August 843 the Treaty of Verdun divided the Frankish Empire into three kingdoms. Lothair received the imperial title and direct rule over a strip of land from Frisia to Italy, known as Middle Francia; Louis the German inherited the East Frankish kingdom stretching from Saxony to Bavaria, while Charles the Bald gained West Francia. While East Francia and West Francia were relatively defensible, Middle Francia, bisected as it was by the Alps, suffered from poor internal communications and was particularly difficult to defend against the incursions of the Vikings and others. This political fragmentation, coupled with the increase in the size of Viking fleets, ushered in a new period of large-scale Viking attacks in Francia.

MAP KEY

1 25 June 841: The battle of Fontenoy sees Frankish forces led by Lothair I and his nephew Pepin II defeated by troops commanded by Louis the German and Charles the Bald.

2 24 June 843: A Viking fleet numbering 67 ships attacks Nantes.

3 August 843: The Treaty of Verdun divides the Frankish Empire into three: Middle Francia (Lothair), East Francia (Louis the German) and West Francia (Charles the Bald).

4 844: Pepin II invites the Viking adventurer Oscar to attack Toulouse via the River Garonne.

5 845: Vikings sack Hamburg, a major Frankish missionary centre, and destroy its cathedral.

6 29 March 845: After plundering the Seine Valley, a 120-vessel fleet under Ragnar Lothbrok attacks Paris on Easter Sunday, plundering and occupying the city. Charles the Bald pays the Vikings 7,000lb of silver in tribute and they withdraw.

7 22 November 845: The Breton ruler Nominoë's forces defeat Charles the Bald's men at Ballon.

8 847: Oscar's Vikings seize Bordeaux, the capital of Aquitaine.

9 22 August 851: The Breton victory at Jengland leads to the Treaty of Angers. The Breton ruler receives the title of king while acknowledging Charles the Bald as his overlord.

10 852: A Danish contingent under Godfrid, son of Harald Klak, plunders Frisia and Flanders and then establishes a winter camp at Jeufosse. Charles the Bald's Franks surround the Northmen's camp, but refuse to prosecute their attack.

11 September 855: The Treaty of Prüm sees Lothair I divide his realm into three: Italy (Louis the Younger), Lotharingia (Lothair II) and Provence (Charles).

12 856: Charles the Bald defeats a Viking contingent in the forest of Perche.

13 28 December 856: The Vikings sack Paris for a second time.

14 858: Charles the Bald's royal host besieges the Viking base at Oissel, but Louis the German's invasion of West Francia prompts Charles's men to suspend their operations in September. In 861, after being paid by Charles the Bald, Vikings under Weland besiege the Northmen encamped at Oissel; negotiations between the two factions result in all of the Scandinavians leaving the island, only reaching the Frankish coast in the spring of 862.

15 862: Charles the Bald's men trap a Viking force by blocking a bridge across the River Marne at Isles-lès-Villenoy. The Franks construct fortifications at nearby Pont-de-l'Arche.

16 January 863: Following the death of Charles of Provence, his kingdom is divided between those of Louis the Younger and Lothair II.

17 866: After a Viking contingent bypasses Pont-de-l'Arche and heads along the River Seine towards Paris, Frankish forces led by Robert the Strong attempt to defeat them at Melun, but are put to flight. Frankish attempts to block the Seine at Pîtres by constructing fortifications are unable to prevent the Vikings from returning along the river.

18 2 July 866: On their way back to the River Loire from sacking Le Mans, a 400-strong Breton–Viking force encounters and defeats a Frankish army at Brissarthe; Robert the Strong is killed.

19 August 870: The Treaty of Meerssen partitions Lotharingia between Louis the German and Charles the Bald, leaving three kingdoms: East Francia, West Francia and Italy.

20 873: A Frankish army commanded by Charles the Bald surrounds and besieges the Viking encampment at Angers. The Vikings commend themselves to Charles the Bald and promise to leave his kingdom if they are permitted to stay on a small island in the Loire until February, so that they can hold a market there. Charles grants the Vikings' request, and they withdraw to the Loire.

Battlefield environment

Although it was not yet the capital city it would eventually become, Viking Age Paris was an important centre of religion and commerce. One of the many market towns along the River Seine, the city was involved in the lucrative wine trade and benefited from the proximity of the wealthy monasteries of Saint-Denis and Saint-Germain-des-Prés – but the influx of wealth generated through trade and the treasures of local monasteries made Paris a tempting target for a Viking attack.

Like many Frankish towns, Angers was built near navigable waterways, providing easy access to Scandinavian raiders. Angers was especially vulnerable, lying as it did near the border between Brittany and Normandy. Most notably, Angers would be the location of one of the few encounters in which the Vikings were besieged. Similarly, Brissarthe, located in the fertile Loire Valley region, appears to have been the perfect environment for a Viking assault.

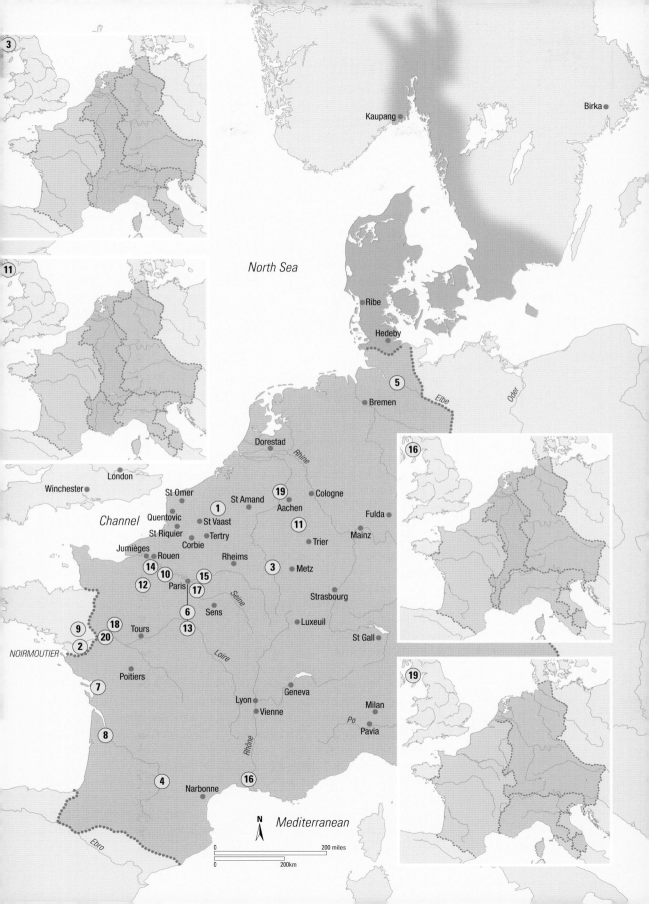

North Sea

Kaupang

Birka

Ribe

Hedeby

⑤

Bremen

Elbe

Oder

③

⑪

Dorestad

Rhine

London

Winchester

St Omer

St Amand

⑲

Cologne

Channel

Quentovic

①

St Vaast

Aachen

Fulda

St Riquier

Tertry

⑪

Mainz

Jumièges

Corbie

Trier

⑭

Rouen

Rheims

⑫

⑩

Paris

⑮

③

Metz

⑰

Strasbourg

⑥

Sens

Seine

Luxeuil

⑨

⑱

Tours

⑬

St Gall

⑳

②

NOIRMOUTIER

Loire

Poitiers

⑦

Geneva

Lyon

Milan

⑧

Vienne

Po

Pavia

④

Narbonne

⑯

Rhône

N

Mediterranean

Ebro

⑯

⑲

0		200 miles
0		200km

INTO COMBAT

The strife in Francia during the early 840s heralded the most intense period of Viking activity in the realms of Charlemagne's heirs. In 841 the Vikings moved along the River Seine and sacked Rouen; the city would be at the centre of Viking activities in West Francia for decades to come. In 842 it was the turn of Quentovic, the long-established Frankish trading post, thereby sealing its long-term demise. The Viking contingent responsible for looting Quentovic made their winter camp on an island in the mouth of the River Loire, then moved up the River Garonne in 844 and sacked Toulouse, before sailing along the Iberian coast and attacking several Christian and Muslim settlements (Collins 1999: 371).

The turmoil in Francia also led to a reassertion of Breton strength in the north-western part of West Francia. Three battles served to cement the Bretons' claim to determine their own future, free from Frankish interference. On 24 May 843 the battle of Blain, also known as Messac, pitted Breton forces against their erstwhile Frankish overlords in a clash that saw the Franks decisively beaten; a Viking contingent led by Hastein may have also been involved in the latter stages of the battle, but this is unclear (Nelson 1991: 55). The battle of Ballon on 22 November 845 saw the Bretons under their leader Nominoë, a longstanding ally of Louis the Pious, defeat Frankish forces loyal to Charles the Bald, thereby reinforcing the Breton bid for independence from their Frankish neighbours. The battle of Jengland on 22 August 851, yet another Breton victory, would lead that September to the Treaty of Angers, by which Nominoë received the title of king while notionally recognizing Charles as his overlord; the Breton March gave way to a consolidated and expanded Breton kingdom that was better able to defend itself against the Vikings.

A third consequence of the strife in Francia was an apparent shift in the stance of the Danish king, Horik I (r. 813–54), towards the Franks. Although Horik was intermittently receptive to the East Franks' efforts to spread the Christian faith among the Danes, a Viking contingent sacked Hamburg in 845 and destroyed its cathedral – a centre for Frankish missionary efforts in Scandinavia – before attempting to move further along the River Elbe, only to be defeated (Collins 1999: 372). It is unclear whether Horik tacitly approved the Viking expeditions that targeted Paris, Hamburg and other targets within the Frankish lands, but it is unlikely that he welcomed the prospect of successful Viking raids, as they boosted the prestige of those Northmen who participated in them.

Since the time of Louis the Pious, the nature of Viking attacks had changed dramatically. The raiders of Louis's time had operated in small fleets, such as the 13 ships rebuffed by the Franks in Flanders in 820, or the nine that attacked Noirmoutier in 835 (Coupland 2004: 51). By 843, Viking fleets were no longer modest in size, however. A Scandinavian fleet that attacked Nantes in that year numbered 67 vessels; and two years later, a mighty fleet of 120 longships sailed along the Seine under the leadership of a man called Ragnar. This leader has come to be identified as Ragnar Lothbrok, a semi-legendary figure mentioned in the Old Norse sagas.

In March 845, in the absence of organized Frankish resistance, Ragnar and his Northmen sailed up the Seine to Paris, laying waste to everything

The emperor Lothair I is seated on a throne wearing a crown and accompanied by two guards in this depiction from the *Gospels of Lothair*, a manuscript made for the emperor himself in Saint-Martin de Tours in 849–51. It represents the peak of the Carolingian-era Tours workshop. (Ann Ronan Pictures/Print Collector/Getty Images)

on either side of the river. The *Annals of Saint-Bertin* describe the brutal Viking attacks along the Seine Valley. In an effort to defeat the raiders, Charles the Bald stationed Frankish troops along both sides of the Seine. Ragnar attacked the smaller of these two Frankish contingents with the whole of his army, estimated to have been 3,000–4,000 strong. The smaller Frankish force withdrew, but not before Ragnar captured 111 prisoners, whom he hanged along the riverbank in full view of the second Frankish contingent. The remaining Franks understood the Vikings' message and subsequently withdrew.

The Northmen then turned their attentions to Paris, deliberately waiting until Easter Sunday – a day when the city would have been filled with traders, merchants, customers and other visitors as well as the usual population – before launching their attack. The city quickly fell, long before Charles the Bald could counter such a move militarily. In the face of the threat posed by the Bretons, the West Frankish king opted to pay tribute – 7,000lb of silver – to the raiders in exchange for their promise to depart. The Frankish sources related that the raiders were afflicted with widespread disease, which the Frankish chroniclers interpreted as divine retribution upon the despoilers of Paris's holy places.

In the years immediately following the siege of Paris, the Vikings continued to exploit the longstanding divisions among the Frankish elite in the wake of Louis the Pious's death. Having recaptured Aquitaine from Pepin II in 839, Louis the Pious had installed his ally Seguin II as the count of Bordeaux and Saintes. After the battle of Fontenoy, Pepin II returned to Aquitaine, determined to assert his independence from Charles the Bald; but in 844 Pepin made the fateful decision to invite the Viking adventurer Oscar to attack Toulouse via the Garonne.

This replica longship is pictured on the River Spree in Germany in 2014. The mast could be easily lowered and raised thanks to the design of the 'mast fish' and of the mast step in the keelson (a reinforcing structural member atop the keel). While it was useful to be able to lower the mast in many instances, including surprise attacks and covert manoeuvres, the ability to remove the mast meant that longships could pass beneath bridges in many cases. Crucially, longships could operate in shallow waters and be brought ashore on gently sloping beaches. Should an adversary send ships against them, the Vikings could sail or row into shallow waters, making them difficult to engage with. In a land such as Francia, criss-crossed by navigable rivers and estuaries, the Northmen could and did roam free by way of their longships. Longships could also be portaged overland, the vessels being rolled across a series of tree trunks or logs, and returned to the water relatively quickly. (Simone Kuhlmey/Pacific Press/ LightRocket via Getty Images)

An oxbow bend on the Loire. Locations such as this would have been prime sites for Viking encampments. (jeangill/Getty Images)

Having initially transferred his loyalty to Charles the Bald after the death of Louis the Pious, Seguin went over to Pepin II in 845 and was rewarded with the title of duke of Gascony. Seguin marched out against the Viking forces threatening Bordeaux and Saintes, but his army was bested by the Northmen and fled; Seguin himself was captured and put to death in 846. In 847, Oscar's men seized Bordeaux, the capital of Aquitaine, reportedly with the help of disaffected citizens acting on behalf of Pepin. In 848, Charles the Bald's troops attacked the Viking forces at Bordeaux, where the Frankish forces reportedly captured nine enemy ships and slaughtered their crews (Coupland 2004: 58). Pepin was captured by allies of Charles the Bald in 851 or 852 and detained in Soissons; in 854 he escaped and later joined the Vikings established in the Loire Valley, reportedly abandoning his Catholicism and adopting Viking beliefs instead. Captured a second time in 864, he died in captivity at Senlis.

In 852 the Northmen returned to ravage the Low Countries; afterwards, a contingent led by Godfrid, son of Harald Klak, and Sigfrid pitched camp on an island in the Seine opposite Jeufosse, roughly 70km south-west of Rouen and a similar distance away from Paris. Although Charles the Bald invested the Viking camp, his men refused to press home an assault and so he was forced to withdraw his forces at the beginning of 853. That summer, Vikings under Godfrid raided Nantes and Tours on the Loire (Haywood 2016: 88–89).

On 19 September 855, suffering from poor health and aware that his life was coming to an end, Lothair I decided to divide Middle Francia between his three sons. Louis 'the Younger' (825–75) was to receive the imperial crown and the Kingdom of Italy; Lothair II (835–69) was to rule over Frisia and parts of Austrasia, an area that subsequently became known as Lotharingia; and Charles (845–63) was to be king of Provence. Lothair I himself abdicated and retired to Prüm Abbey, where he died on 29 September 855. There were now no fewer than five distinct Frankish kingdoms; this fluid situation would evolve further as various monarchs died and the successions became disputed.

In 856, a Frankish force led by Charles the Bald defeated a Viking force in the forest of Perche (Coupland 2004: 58–59). The Northmen returned to the Seine that August, plundering as they went, and once again wintered

River encounter

Frankish view: A Frankish scouting party stumbles upon a group of Vikings retreating from their island encampment. Supported by a dismounted archer, the mounted Franks bear winged lances, helpful in harassing the enemy while engaging them from a distance. One scout sounds a horn, alerting nearby troops. Though outnumbered, the Franks possess the high ground and understand that the Vikings intend to flee with their booty. Hoping to liberate the captive clergymen, and to take back the portable items the Vikings have purloined, the Franks await reinforcements. The Frankish scouts, some wearing the iconic Frankish helmet which slopes down the wearer's neck, are clad in scale armour, wearing linen beneath this. Small-scale skirmishes such as the one depicted here were common in Viking Age Francia.

Viking view: The Vikings quickly move to the safety of their longship, keen to avoid combat to protect their lucrative plunder, which includes human cargo. Not expecting to encounter the detachment of Franks close to their island base, the Vikings are lightly equipped, better suited to rapid movement than to pitched battle. The typical Viking helmet, conical in shape, is worn by some of the retreating Northmen. Wearing a Gjermundbu-style helmet, with a spectacle-shaped facial guard and mail aventail intended to protect his neck, a well-armoured Viking chieftain is ordering his men to fall back to the safety of their longship. A mounted member of the chieftain's retinue is struck by an arrow in the heart, killing him instantly and causing him to drop a sack of valuable loot.

at Jeufosse. On 28 December 856, the Vikings sacked Paris for a second time. This time the raiders must have opened negotiations with at least some of the city's leading men, for treasure covertly changed hands and three of Paris's churches were spared the flames when the Vikings set the city alight (Haywood 2016: 89). The Vikings also extracted a colossal ransom from the West Frankish king in exchange for the return of two high-profile hostages captured during the second Paris raid – Louis, abbot of Saint-Denis and his half-brother Gauzlin. These two clerics were at the centre of West Frankish politics, with Louis serving as Charles the Bald's arch-chancellor and Gauzlin being appointed the bishop of Paris shortly before the fateful siege of 885–86 (see page 65).

Perhaps wary of becoming vulnerable by remaining at Jeufosse – or possibly seeking new opportunities – the Northmen now relocated their base on the Seine to Oissel, an island much closer to Rouen. Here they were besieged once again by the Frankish royal host during the summer of 858, but the threat posed to Charles the Bald by Louis the German's invasion of West Frankish territory forced the besiegers to suspend their operations that September. Instead, Charles turned to another Viking leader to solve the problem.

In 860, Charles the Bald entered into an agreement with a Viking leader named Weland who had been active along the River Somme. After Charles paid Weland an initial instalment of 3,000lb of silver the Northman took his warriors to Oissel, where he besieged the Vikings there in 861. Charles strove to avoid Weland's men plundering the Seine Valley by instructing the locals to provide the Scandinavians with supplies. Weland's blockade and the ensuing hardships among the besieged induced the Oissel Vikings to open negotiations, handing 6,000lb of loot to Weland. The Vikings all decided to leave Oissel, but the onset of poor weather drove them into winter quarters along the length of the Seine. It was only in the spring of 862 that the Vikings finally reached the coast and dispersed (Haywood 2016: 90).

In 862, keen to avoid yet more Viking depredations in the royal estates, Charles the Bald managed to trap a Viking fleet by blocking a bridge across the River Marne at Isles-lès-Villenoy and deploying troops along the bank as usual. The Vikings were forced into submission, and the Franks constructed fortifications at nearby Pont-de-l'Arche, with the intent of barring Viking passage along the river. Forts of stone, timber and earth were planned at either end of the bridge for the purpose of housing garrisons of Frankish troops. Additional bridges were to be constructed along the Oise, Loire and Marne to increase Frankish mobility and act as temporary barriers.

The critical weakness of Charles the Bald's fortified bridges ploy was exposed in 865, however, when a new Viking fleet entered the Seine. The Frankish garrison failed to meet the threat in time, and when the Northmen fell upon another detachment, the Frankish warriors turned and fled. While appearing a sound defensive tactic, the use of fortified bridges was not very effective against the Vikings, and Charles the Bald's successors seem to have abandoned this ploy entirely. It had succeeded on one notable occasion, but consistently failed because of the logistical impracticality of closing off the

Appearing with inlaid inscriptions, Frankish swords often bore the name 'Ulfberht', denoting a sort of medieval trademark among European swordsmiths of the Early Middle Ages. The spelling of this name and the quality of the sword blades varied throughout the Middle Ages, suggesting that a popular maker's mark may have been copied by aspiring swordsmiths (Williams 2019: 18). (BEN STANSALL/AFP via Getty Images)

waterways that brought wealth and trade into the heartland of West Francia. Barriers such as these blocked Frankish rivers – the commercial arteries of the medieval world – and were therefore only deployed temporarily. This explains how Viking fleets bypassed the fortifications at Pont-de-l'Arche in 865 and went on to camp on an island near Paris.

The year 866 saw a decisive victory for Vikings who marauded along the Seine. The Northmen sailed right along Francia's most important waterway to the Frankish fortress at Melun. Charles the Bald deployed cavalry squadrons to advance along both sides of the Seine. The Vikings disembarked to attack what appeared to be the larger and stronger squadron, commanded by the Frankish leader Robert the Strong and his long-time ally, Odo, formerly count of Troyes (Nelson 1991: 129–30). Robert the Strong, an acclaimed military leader who had fought against the Vikings on numerous occasions, had been made a royal official by Charles the Bald and was the great-grandfather of Hugh Capet, a future Frankish king.

The *Annals of Saint-Bertin* relate that the Northmen put the Frankish defenders to flight without a battle, and returned with their ships loaded with booty. To make matters worse, the Vikings forced Charles the Bald to pay 4,000lb of silver as tribute in exchange for peace. To raise such a large sum, the Frankish king taxed his subjects, who were already expected to pay handsomely so that their realm might muster a royal host adequate to oppose the Vikings. Furthermore, the Franks were forced to release all of their Scandinavian prisoners and pay compensation for some of the Vikings they had killed.

The Northmen then moved on from Melun down the Seine until they reached a place suitable for making repairs to their ships and constructing new ones. An abortive attempt to confine these Vikings failed after Charles the Bald marched to a place called Pîtres with workmen and carts to fortify the Seine so that the Vikings might not be able to sail further along the river beyond that point. In July 866, only one month after the Franks began building these fortifications, the Viking army departed from their island base and sailed upon the open sea.

The year 866 would soon witness a further Frankish defeat at the hands of the Northmen. Salomon, the duke of Brittany, made contact with the Viking leader Hastein to form an alliance against their common enemy: Charles the Bald's West Francia. (Salomon had assumed his ducal title in November 857, having assassinated his cousin Erispoe, the victor at Jengland in 851.) For his part, Robert the Strong had also concluded alliances with parties of Northmen in his efforts to defeat the Bretons. The conflict between the Franks and their Breton neighbours was a complex and drawn-out struggle, with double-dealing on both sides; the Vikings saw the possibility of profit and parties of Northmen fought on both sides at different times.

In 866 a Breton–Danish force attacked Poitou, Anjou, Maine and Touraine, laying waste to the surrounding areas. According to the *Annals of Saint-Bertin*, about 400 Vikings, along with a contingent of Bretons, came up from the Loire with their horses to attack the city of Le Mans (Nelson 1991: 135). On their way back, they encountered a Frankish contingent at Brissarthe on 2 July 866. The Franks pursued the Vikings, who sought refuge in a church; Robert the Strong's men surrounded the building. That night, as the Northmen attempted to escape under cover of darkness, they killed Robert and mortally wounded Ranulf I, duke of Aquitaine; the Franks retreated and the Vikings escaped.

Following the death of Charles, king of Provence, on 25 January 863, his realm had been divided between Louis the Younger, emperor and king of Italy, and Lothair II. Further Frankish consolidation occurred in the wake of Lothair II's death on 8 August 869; exactly one year later, the Treaty of Meerssen partitioned Lotharingia between Louis the Pious's two surviving sons, Louis the German and Charles the Bald, leaving only three kingdoms: East Francia, West Francia and Italy.

The Loire Valley endured the depredations of the Vikings in the years before 873, with the invaders wreaking havoc on the towns, villages and farms in the region. A Viking contingent led by Hastein had been established at Angers for some time when in 873, according to the *Annals of Saint-Bertin*, Charles the Bald announced that the royal host would advance towards Brittany so that the Northmen occupying Angers could not attack that region and would flee the city for other places where they might be hemmed in and defeated.

Charles the Bald's planned advance into Brittany has been interpreted as a false order given to lure the Vikings based at Angers into a mistaken sense of security. When the Franks came upon the city, they surrounded it with enclosing earthworks, seeking to cut off Viking supply routes and ensure that there was no way forward for the Viking army except through a battle in the open. Though adept in siege warfare, the Franks deployed no siege equipment in their move on Angers. Instead, they sought to starve the Vikings out.

The encounter at Angers is only one of three documented occasions when a Viking army is known to have been besieged. In a siege, the Franks' first priority was typically to surround the enemy, sometimes throwing up a rampart around the fortification as well, as they did at Angers in 873. They would then seek to mount a blockade, preventing any food and water from reaching the besieged force, essentially starving them into submission. A drawn-out investment could, however, also create dangerous problems for the besieging army. Regino of Prüm, who gives a dubious account of the battle at Angers, claimed that the Franks began to run out of food and were struck by sickness. Though historians doubt the authenticity of Regino's report, such situations were not uncommon in contemporary Frankish sieges.

The Viking leaders commended themselves to Charles the Bald and handed over the hostages he demanded. The conditions imposed by the Franks were that, on the appointed day, the Vikings would leave West Francia and never return. The Northmen requested that they be allowed to stay until February 874 on an island in the Loire to hold a market – presumably in order to dispose of the less-portable elements of booty, converting their bulkier 'assets' into food, supplies, gold or silver – and their wish was granted (Nelson 1991: 185). Less dramatic, though more plausible than Regino's account, is the report given in the *Annals of Saint-Bertin* in which the Vikings at Angers were starved into submission.

A pair of Scandinavian, possibly Danish, stirrups, dating from the late 10th or early 11th century. Originally decorated with gilded bronze and silver overlay, these were probably originally deposited in the tomb of a wealthy Viking warrior. Although best known for their maritime exploits, the Vikings were also skilled equestrians and equipment such as stirrups and spurs was often found in Viking burials, alongside weapons or other goods that the deceased wanted to bring to the afterlife. (Sepia Times/ Universal Images Group via Getty Images)

The Later Raids

877–911

BACKGROUND TO BATTLE

The death of Charles the Bald on 6 October 877 started a new round of dynastic wrangling among the Frankish elite that culminated in the emergence of Charles III (839–88; r. 881–87), known as 'the Fat', as the last Carolingian to rule the whole of the Frankish lands. Although his supporters championed him as the new Charlemagne, Charles the Fat would prove singularly ineffective in dealing with his Scandinavian adversaries.

Charles the Fat was the youngest son of Louis the German, the first king of East Francia (r. 843–76). Louis was no stranger to the machinations of power in the Frankish realms; he was involved in his older brothers' revolts against their father, Louis the Pious, in the 860s, helping his brother Carloman to take charge of the duchy of Bavaria in 863 and supporting the uprising mounted by his middle brother, Louis the Younger, in 864. The brothers successfully compelled their father to agree the terms on which his remaining lands were to be divided after his death; Charles was promised Alemannia (part of east Francia) and a portion of Lotharingia.

The emperor Louis II (825–75; r. 855–75) had agreed that Carloman would succeed him as king of Italy, but when Louis II died in August 875, Charles the Bald invaded the Italian peninsula and was crowned king of Italy and emperor that December. In response, Louis the German's forces attacked West Francia, compelling Charles to return from Italy to defend his territory. Louis the German died in August 876, prompting Charles to invade East Francia; this attempt to unite parts of the Frankish lands by force failed at the battle of Andernach on 8 October 876, where Charles was defeated and fled to Italy. When Carloman led East Frankish

forces into Italy in 877, Charles attempted to return to West Francia, but died en route.

Following the death of Charles the Bald, his eldest son Louis (846–79), known as 'the Stammerer', became king of West Francia (r. 866–79) while also retaining the throne of Aquitaine. Plagued by poor health, Louis marched against the Vikings but died on campaign in April 879; his dominions were ruled jointly by his sons Louis III (863–82; r. 879–82) and Carloman II (866–84; r. 879–84). Upon Carloman II's death in December 884, the emperor himself, Charles the Fat, became king of West Francia (r. 884–87); this was the third Frankish kingdom to fall to Charles, as he was already king of Italy and East Francia by this date.

Although Charles the Fat was ruler of all of the Frankish kingdoms, it is important to remember that they remained politically and administratively separate from one another; in no sense was this development a unification of the Frankish lands, despite Charles's efforts to promote the survival of the Carolingian dynasty by commissioning a monk named Notker 'the Stammerer' to write a new life of Charlemagne, called *Gesta Caroli* (Deeds of Charles). Charles was only too well aware that without male heirs, his precarious hold upon all of the Frankish thrones was bound to end with his death.

After being lured away from mainland Europe to concentrate on Britain, the Vikings returned to Francia in 879, driven by the defeat of Guthrum the Old's Great Heathen Army at the hands of Alfred of Wessex's forces at the battle of Edington in May 878, but also attracted by the evident disorder in West Francia in the wake of Charles the Bald's death and the consequent power struggles among the Frankish elite. Thwarted in England, the Vikings appear to have turned back to mainland Europe to continue their search for trade, plunder and conquest. Among other Frankish lands bisected by major rivers, the Seine Valley, which had been largely ignored by the Northmen since the mid-860s, would once again be the setting for Viking depredations.

A selection of Anglo-Saxon weapons: three spears, a sword and an iron shield-boss. Viking raiding and settlement in Francia must be seen in the context of their contemporaneous activities in the Anglo-Saxon realms, Ireland and further afield. In the wake of his defeat at Edington in May 878, Guthrum the Old agreed to be baptized and acceded to the terms of the Treaty of Wedmore, which required him to return to East Anglia. Guthrum's forces appear to have travelled with him, but it seems that another Viking host made its way up the River Thames and camped at Fulham during the winter of 879/80. In any event, Guthrum the Old remained king of East Anglia until his death in about 890, and although the West Saxons and the Vikings continued to spar over the boundary between the two polities, Alfred's military reforms kept the Danes at bay. (Museum of London/Heritage Images/ Getty Images)

MAP KEY

1 February 880: Louis III and Carloman II, the joint rulers of West Francia, and Louis the Younger, king of Saxony and Bavaria, sign the Treaty of Ribemont, the final partition of the Frankish Empire before Charles the Fat inherits West Francia and thus becomes the sole ruler of Francia in 884.

2 February 880: Louis the Younger defeats a Viking force at Thimeon.

3 3 August 881: West Frankish troops defeat Vikings at Saucourt-en-Vimeu.

4 11 April 882: After sacking Trier, a Viking band led by Godfrid and Sigfrid defeats a Frankish force at Remich; Wala, the archbishop of Metz, is killed.

5 July 882: Charles the Fat lays siege to the Viking base at Asselt; the siege ends in negotiations, with Godfrid submitting to the emperor while Sigfrid leaves following the payment of tribute.

6 June 885: A Frankish contingent attacks the Viking camp at Rouen, but withdraws after Ragnold, duke of Le Mans, is killed.

7 November 885–October 886: A massive Viking army sails up the River Seine and lays siege to Paris. After nearly a year of inconclusive siege operations, Charles the Fat agrees to pay the Vikings tribute, and allows them to plunder further along the Seine.

8 November 887: Word reaches Charles the Fat, based at Frankfurt am Main, of the revolt of Arnulf of Carinthia in East Francia. Days later, Charles is deposed and agrees to retire to Swabia, dying in January 888.

9 24 June 888: Odo, count of Paris, defeats a Viking contingent at Montfaucon.

10 26 June 891: A Frankish force is defeated near Maastricht; the victorious Vikings make camp at Louvain on the River Dyle.

11 September 891: A Frankish army led by Arnulf dismounts to attack the Viking encampment at Louvain. The Northmen retreat to the Dyle and are decisively defeated.

12 June 911: Viking forces led by Rollo besiege Chartres, defended by Richard of Autun. On 20 July the defenders are relieved by Frankish cavalry led by Charles the Simple. The two sides enter negotiations that result in the Treaty of Saint-Clair-sur-Epte.

Battlefield environment

The Vikings active in Francia continued to pursue their well-established raiding tactics in the closing years of the 9th century, by which time they had identified a number of suitable bases that offered the raiders access to Francia's major cities, monasteries and other sources of portable wealth. In 885–86 the Vikings mounted their most formidable assault on Paris, but were unable to overcome the defenders in a siege that lasted for nearly a year.

The settlement referred to as *Ascloha* in the chronicles is now associated with Asselt, near Roemond in the Netherlands. Asselt would be a thorn in the flesh of the East Frankish rulers, but it was Rouen in West Francia that proved to be the basis for long-term Scandinavian settlement in the Frankish lands.

A view of the Square du Vert-Galant, at the heart of present-day Paris. It seems that the only way to gain access into Viking Age Paris was via the Grand-Pont and Petit Pont bridges and their fortified towers that blockaded the Seine in two locations. These bridges limited the Vikings' mobility and forced them to spend their energy and resources attacking these fortified points before ever reaching the city itself. (pawel.gaul/ Getty Images)

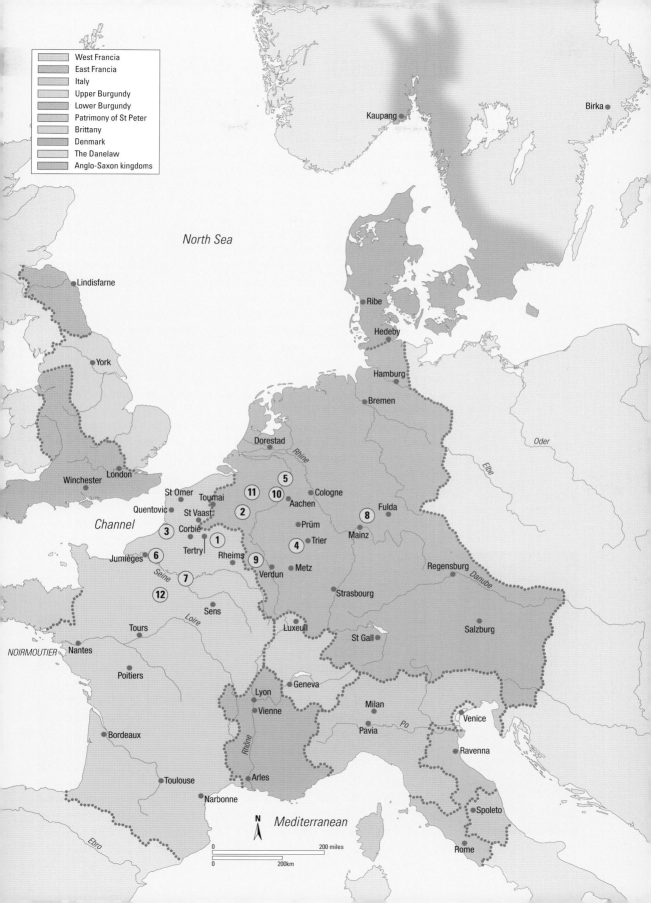

Legend

	West Francia
	East Francia
	Italy
	Upper Burgundy
	Lower Burgundy
	Patrimony of St Peter
	Brittany
	Denmark
	The Danelaw
	Anglo-Saxon kingdoms

North Sea

Kaupang

Birka

Lindisfarne

York

Ribe

Hedeby

Hamburg

Bremen

Dorestad

Rhine

Oder

Elbe

Winchester

London

Channel

St Omer

Tournai

Quentovic

St Vaast

(11)

(10)

(5)

Cologne

Aachen

Fulda

Corbie

(2)

Prüm

(8)

Mainz

(3)

(1)

(4)

Trier

Tertry

Rheims

(9)

Jumièges

(6)

Metz

Regensburg

Danube

Verdun

(7)

Strasbourg

(12)

Seine

Sens

Loire

Luxeuil

St Gall

Salzburg

Tours

Nantes

NOIRMOUTIER

Poitiers

Geneva

Lyon

Milan

Venice

Vienne

Po

Bordeaux

Pavia

Ravenna

Toulouse

Rhône

Arles

Narbonne

Spoleto

Ebro

N

Mediterranean

Rome

| 0 | 200 miles |
| 0 | 200km |

INTO COMBAT

Following the death of Louis the Stammerer in April 879, Viking activity in Francia appears to have increased (Collins 1999: 375). Vikings were reported to be active in various locations across the Frankish realms, including Ghent in 879, Courtrai and Saxony in 880, Aachen – where they ransacked Charlemagne's palace – and Amiens in 881 and 883, the siege of Asselt in 882, Condé on the River Scheldt in 882, and Louvain in 884 (Davis 1988: 157). A contingent of Northmen attacked Thérouanne on the River Lys and raided into the Scheldt Valley and Brabant. In 881 they looted the monasteries of Saint-Vaast, Saint-Riquier and Corbie.

The Frankish kings were not idle in the face of this renewed threat. In February 880 Louis the Younger (830–82), the king of Saxony and Bavaria (r. 876–82) and the second son of Louis the German, defeated the Vikings at Thimeon, his own son Hugh being killed in the fighting (McKitterick 1995: 234–35). West Frankish forces reportedly won a victory against the Northmen at Saucourt-en-Vimeu on 3 August 881, with the anonymous author of the *Ludwigslied* (The Lay of Ludwig) claiming that 8,000 Vikings were killed. As on so many occasions, however, these Frankish victories were hollow; they could not defeat the invaders decisively, and in the wake of the encounter at Saucourt-en-Vimeu the city of Rheims was ransacked by the Vikings in 882, its archbishop, Hincmar, forced to flee (Collins 1999: 375).

After spending the winter of 881/82 at Asselt, a Viking band led by Godfrid and Sigfrid conducted raiding operations along the rivers Moselle and Rhone. On 5 April the Northmen captured the city of Trier, the Easter festivities doubtless meaning that the city was full of visitors. Bertulf, the archbishop of Trier, escaped with a handful of his men; the Vikings departed with their booty. Although a Frankish contingent led by Bertulf alongside Wala, the archbishop of Metz, and Adalhard, count of Metz, confronted the raiders at Remich on 11 April, the Franks were defeated; Wala was killed in the fighting. Despite prevailing in the battle, the Vikings returned to Asselt; there they would be besieged by Charles the Fat in July 882 (Nelson 1991: 224).

Two continuations of the *Annals of Fulda* each provide a different account of the siege of Asselt (Coupland 2004: 66). One source suggests that the Northmen were on the point of capitulating when the Frankish leadership allowed them to escape their fate by concluding a deal; the other (more plausible) account remarks upon the decaying corpses that had spread sickness among the besiegers – a common occurrence in siege warfare, with troops concentrated in a particular area for a prolonged period. In any case, both of these sources agree on the outcome of the negotiations: Godfrid submitted to Charles the Fat, while Sigfrid left following the payment of tribute.

Moving south along the River Seine, a contingent of Vikings built a fortified camp on the riverbank opposite Rouen. A Frankish force attacked the Vikings at Rouen in June 885, but withdrew after Ragnold, duke of Le Mans, was killed with several of his men. The Vikings moved further south and burned the Frankish fortress at Pontoise, intended to deny the Northmen passage along the River Oise.

Charles the Fat, depicted here as part of the 13th-century Charlemagne Shrine at Aachen, was King of the Franks during 881–88, having reigned solely over West Francia from 884 onwards. He was the great-grandson of Charlemagne and the last legitimate Carolingian monarch to rule over the entire Frankish realm. His lack of support for the besieged defenders of Paris in 885–86 damaged his reputation, however. After some uncertainty and hesitation, Charles did lift the siege of Paris by paying tribute to the Viking invaders. This action led to his unpopularity and subsequent downfall after many Franks felt their dogged defence of the city had been in vain. With the exception of Charlemagne, the defence of Francia against the Vikings seemed to be better off in the hands of local leaders, not Carolingian monarchs. (DEA/G. DAGLI ORTI/Getty Images)

On 24 November 885, the Vikings arrived once again at the outskirts of Paris with a substantial host. The events of the next year would mark a turning point in the Frankish struggle against the Vikings, as the two sides became bogged down in a brutal 11-month siege that would test the limits of both Viking and Frankish warriors. The account of the siege attributed to Abbo of Saint-Germain-des-Prés, known as the *Bella Parisiacæ urbis* (Wars of the City of Paris), states that the Viking fleet numbered at least 700 ships and carried a force of some 40,000 men – clearly an implausible total – while the Frankish defenders numbered just 200. This time, however, the Franks had the advantage of substantial fortifications, constructed or substantially improved since the raids of the 840s and 850s. They also had two leaders – former Viking captive Gauzlin, now bishop of Paris, and Odo, son of Robert the Strong and count of Paris – who were determined to resist, rather than allow the Scandinavians to plunder their homes or move past the city towards the prosperous lands upstream.

The day after the Viking armada arrived, Sigfrid met Gauzlin and asked that his fleet might travel past Paris and conduct raiding operations beyond the city, but the cleric refused. On the morning of 25 November, the Northmen targeted the tower at Grand-Pont. This tower blocked access to Paris via the wooden bridge, which connected the northern (right) bank of the Seine to the island on which the city was built. The Vikings came against it with their siege engines – reportedly, catapults, battering-rams and fire-ships (i.e. longships that were set alight and driven into structures in a bid to set them on fire) – and assailed it with volleys of arrows. The Franks resisted stoutly, pouring boiling oil on the attackers and employing their own siege engines. The assault continued on 26 November, but again the tower did not fall to the attackers.

The Vikings now adjusted their approach, establishing a camp at the abbey of Saint-Germain l'Auxerrois on the northern bank of the Seine. On 31 January 886, the attackers launched a three-pronged assault on the Grand-Pont; a savage but inconclusive three-day battle ensued, with the deadlock only broken when the Seine flooded on 6 February, resulting in the destruction of the Petit Pont and the isolation of the Frankish tower on the southern bank. By now desperate, the defenders sent word to Henry, duke of the Austrasians, Charles the Fat's senior military commander and an implacable foe of the Northmen. Veterans of many battles against the Vikings in East Francia, Henry's forces attempted to relieve the Frankish garrison, but were unable to storm the Viking camp.

The Northmen could now move past Paris along the Seine as they had wished; some of the Vikings continued to prosecute the siege but others moved on in search of other opportunities further afield. Sigfrid himself departed after receiving 60lb of silver, but many Vikings did not, and the siege continued. By the spring of 886, the hungry Frankish garrison were ravaged by pestilence, with Gauzlin himself dying on 16 April. Count Odo secretly left Paris and rode to meet Charles the Fat, begging him to personally lead an army to lift the siege. Having received no firm assurances, on his return to the beleaguered city Odo and his escort were ambushed but regained the safety of Paris.

Months later, in October 886, Charles the Fat finally raised an army and approached Paris; Henry, his commander-in-chief, lost his life en route.

Given the close-quarters nature of siege fighting along walls and atop teetering ladders, swords would have suited the Viking attackers well. This Viking Age sword was found in York and is of a characteristically Scandinavian design. (CM Dixon/Print Collector/ Getty Images)

After nearly a year of suffering, the Frankish garrison learned that Charles had attempted to resolve the situation by agreeing to the Vikings' original demand and paying the raiders 700lb of silver to leave the region. After porting their longships overland and re-entering the Seine beyond Paris, the Northmen duly moved into Burgundy and sacked the abbey of Luxeuil (Davis 1988: 157).

Following Charles's ignominious behaviour in the face of the Vikings besieging Paris, he appears to have suffered a health crisis of some sort (Collins 1999: 358). Charles had already had his efforts to have his illegitimate son Bernard recognized as his heir rebuffed by his bishops. Under pressure, Charles adopted Louis of Provence (880–928), known as 'the Blind' – the illegitimate son of a former usurper, Boso – as his heir. This act likely sealed his fate. In November 887, Charles was at Frankfurt am Main when he received news that his nephew, Arnulf of Carinthia (c.850–99), had raised the standard of revolt in East Francia. Only days later, Charles was deposed as the ruler of East Francia, Lotharingia and the Kingdom of Italy, and agreed to retire to Swabia. Charles died shortly afterwards, on 13 January 888; the Frankish lands fragmented into five kingdoms and would remain separate for nearly 1,000 years until they were briefly reunited under Napoleon.

In the wake of Arnulf's rebellion and Charles the Fat's death, the Franks descended once more into fighting among themselves. Each part of the Frankish lands elected a king, with elements of the West Franks choosing Odo, count of Paris. Odo, who was hampered in his claim by the fact that he was not of Carolingian descent, immediately faced opposition, however – not only from Guy, duke of Spoleto, who was crowned king of Italy in 889 and emperor in 891, but also from a variety of regional magnates. In Provence, Charles's protégé Louis the Blind (c.880–928) became king (r. 887–928), a move subsequently endorsed by Arnulf. In Upper Burgundy, Duke Rudolph (859–912) was made king (r. 889–912), having failed to claim the whole of Burgundy in the face of Arnulf's opposition. In Aquitaine, Duke Ranulf (850–90) proclaimed himself king of that region and refused to recognize Odo's claim, instead advancing the claim of the Carolingian Charles the Simple (879–929; r. 898–922); in the event, Aquitaine passed to Odo only after Ranulf's death. Odo recognized Arnulf's primacy and paid homage to him in 888, but although Odo continued to tackle the Viking threat – reportedly defeating a force of Northmen at Montfaucon, between the rivers Aisne and Meuse, on 24 June 888 – the West Frankish king's grip on power was hampered by the fact that he was not a Carolingian.

Amid this storm of competing factions, Arnulf of Carinthia was campaigning against the Slavs on the Bavarian frontier in June 891 when Frankish forces confronted a force of Vikings moving through Lotharingia. Arnulf had instructed his troops to prevent the Northmen from crossing the Meuse, but they were too slow to prevent the Vikings from crossing the river near Liége and moving into the vicinity of Aachen. Regino of Prüm tells us (Davis 1988: 165–66) that the Northmen killed all those they encountered and captured supplies intended for the Frankish host sent to defeat them. On 24 June, the Frankish army's leaders met to discuss what to do; unsure of the Vikings' intentions, they made no move that day, but on the following morning headed downstream to meet the Northmen in battle.

Reaching a stream called the Geule, about 8km from Maastricht, the Frankish army formed up on 26 June and opted to send small detachments of scouts out to reconnoitre (Davis 1988: 165). Before they could do so, however, Viking scouting parties were spotted and the main Frankish host rushed to engage them, losing its formation in the process. When the over-confident Franks blundered into the village held by the Viking main body, carefully assembled in a defensive circle, the Franks were quickly forced back. The Viking foot soldiers raised a great din, shouting and beating on their quivers (David 1988: 165), thereby summoning a force of mounted Vikings that charged the Franks and drove them back in disorder. As the Franks fled the field, the Vikings pursued them, killing many of the Frankish leaders and capturing much booty. Glutted with plunder in the wake of their victory, the Viking contingent set up a fortified camp at Louvain, unopposed, with a swamp on one side and the River Dyle on the other. Such an inaccessible location appears to have been chosen precisely to hinder the deployment of the Frankish cavalry.

When news of this humiliation reached Arnulf, he mourned the loss of life and also of Frankish prestige. Determined to restore Frankish honour and defeat the Northmen, he assembled an army and headed towards the Norsemen's encampment. Arnulf's army hesitated to close on the Vikings, however, because the situation of the enemy camp gave his mounted warriors no chance to attack. Frankish chroniclers state that Arnulf's warriors were unused to fighting on foot, but were compelled to do so in order to attack the Viking camp (Reuter 1992: 122). As Arnulf's army arrived at Louvain on

The interior of Charlemagne's church at Aachen displays the wealth and power of the Carolingian Empire at its peak. Charlemagne began construction of the church in the late 8th century, with the help of his architect Odo of Metz. In a letter, Alcuin of York reveals that construction was progressing in 798; the date of its final completion is unknown. Upon his death in 814, Charlemagne was buried within the church. Viking raiders are said to have stabled their horses in this building in 881 (Nelson 1997: 30). (Insights/Universal Images Group via Getty Images)

Arnulf of Carinthia

Arnulf (c.850–8 December 899) was the nephew of Charles the Fat, being the illegitimate son of the Frankish king's brother Carloman. Arnulf won a formidable military reputation in campaigns against the Moravians and others. In November 887, he led a coup against his uncle, who had ignored him as a potential heir. Charles was overthrown by Arnulf at a convention in Tribur. The emperor's men deserted him, and the sick, ageing monarch was ordered to Alemannia, where Arnulf had granted him a pension consisting of multiple estates (Costambeys, Innes & MacLean 2011: 424–25). Like so many of his fellow Frankish monarchs, Arnulf spent his life in the saddle amid incessant campaigning, notably in Italy, before ill-health rendered him incapable of countering the growing threat from the Magyars and maintaining primacy within the Empire. He was succeeded in East Francia by his son Louis the Child (r. 900–11). For centuries, it was asserted that no one other than a male Carolingian could rule in Francia. Arnulf's rise to power, however, paved the way for non-Carolingian elites to hold high offices, such as Odo, the count of Paris who became king of West Francia (r. 888–98).

horseback, the general impression is that the host was indeed predominantly mounted (Coupland 2004: 62).

The *Annals of Fulda* ascribe great significance to the ensuing battle at Louvain. While looking upon the Viking camp, which had been fortified with a surrounding ditch, Arnulf and his key subordinates considered how the Frankish army would engage the Northmen in their encampment. The *Annals of Fulda* relate that Arnulf addressed his men and stirred them up with a great speech, commanding them to avenge the blood of their relatives (Reuter 1992: 122). Upon hearing this speech, Frankish warriors, young and old, were equally urged to fight the battle on foot. After Arnulf opted to deploy a force of cavalry in the Frankish rear, lest the Vikings attack from that direction, the two sides commenced the usual preparations for combat, raising great shouts of defiance, parading battle standards and readying their weapons (Reuter 1992: 122).

The battle at Louvain ended in a defeat for the Vikings, who had fled to the Dyle as though it had been a safe 'wall' to their rear. Instead, writes the Frankish chronicler, it would be their downfall. Grasping each other in heaps by hand, neck and limbs, many of the Vikings sank into the river, their dead bodies blocking it entirely, according to one account. While this statement might be one Frankish chronicler's exaggeration, it may not be so far from the truth. According to Ramon Kenis, secretary of the Louvain Historical Society, the Dyle is not more than about 5–7m wide and 1m deep today, as it probably was in 891 (Apelblat 2016). Whether the Vikings had been able to house their longships – which could measure 20–30m in length and 4–5m in width – along this river in light of its narrowness and lack of depth is unclear. While the Vikings may have intended to use such a river to their strategic advantage, its given narrowness may have disordered any retreating warriors, making them especially vulnerable to attack from the shore. The riverbanks are steep, and although the Vikings thought the Dyle to be a defensible 'wall' protecting their camp to the rear, it turned out to be a nightmare in which many Scandinavians were trapped during their retreat from the battle.

The *Annals of Fulda* also relate that Sigfrid and Godfrid were both killed during the battle, and no fewer than 16 royal standards were carried off to

Rollo of Normandy

Little firm information is known of Rollo (*c.*860–*c.*930), a Viking chieftain who led his followers in raiding and pillaging from his base at Rouen, near Paris. In 911, he entered into negotiations with Charles the Simple at Saint-Clair-sur-Epte. While the exact terms of the agreement reached are unknown, a peace treaty was signed: Rollo was granted the countship of Rouen, converted to Christianity, and promised to defend the Seine Valley against other Scandinavian raiders. In terms of his domain, Rollo was given part of what would eventually become Normandy. At first, his own men and their families would come to settle the region, though more Scandinavians (some of them from England) flocked to the land later known as Normandy. In 922, another Frankish civil war erupted, and Charles the Simple was overthrown. Leveraging the political chaos, Rollo seized the regions of Caen and Bayeux in a campaign that would double the size of his domain (Haywood 2016: 101). Rollo's legacy would be the duchy of Normandy, its high point coming with the conquest of England by his descendant William in 1066.

Bavaria as trophies of the Frankish victory (Reuter 1992: 123). Although some chroniclers asserted that nearly all of the Vikings at Louvain were killed or captured, it seems that those Northmen who had stayed with their ships were able to make their escape and headed into East Francia, crossing the Meuse in 892 and raiding the area around Bonn and Prüm (Davis 1988: 166).

While some Frankish chroniclers characterized the battle of Louvain as a decisive defeat for the Vikings that brought peace to the region, others, such as the *Annals of Saint-Vaast*, suggest that the principal reason for the lack of Viking activity around Louvain was a famine that afflicted the area in 892 and prompted the raiders to depart (Coupland & Nelson 1988: 4). The Northmen appear to have stayed away from West Francia until the winter of 896/97 (Collins 1999: 376). After this time, the Vikings resumed their activities in the Loire and Oise valleys and the Seine basin (Coupland & Nelson 1988: 4).

Characteristically, the Frankish elite appear to have taken the temporary cessation of the Viking threat as a signal to begin another round of dynastic fighting (Collins 1999: 376). In 893 Odo was challenged by Charles the Simple, a threat made more potent by Arnulf's decision to back Charles the following year. Odo strove to retain his crown, but after his death in January 898 Charles took the West Frankish throne and reigned until 922, when he was deposed in turn, dying in captivity in October 929.

Despite these dynastic wranglings, however, the West Franks appear to have continued their robust effort to defend their lands, coupled with a new policy of settling the Northmen in vulnerable frontier regions (Collins 1999: 376). In 897 a Frankish force saw off Viking raiders in the Maas Valley and their leader subsequently agreed to be baptized, with Charles the Simple as his godfather. A West Frankish force headed by Richard of Autun defeated Viking raiders in Burgundy in 898, in the wake of Odo's death as West Francia emerged from five years of civil war.

In June 911, the Viking leader Rollo besieged the city of Chartres, defended by forces led by Richard of Autun. On 20 July the defenders were relieved by a contingent of cavalry led by Charles the Simple, which forced the besiegers back towards their ships. In desperation, Rollo opted to slaughter

Odo of France was king of West Francia from 888 to 898 and the first king from the Robertian dynasty. This document pledges Odo's donation to Vic Cathedral in Catalonia for his consecration in 890. (Prisma/UIG/ Getty Images)

A modern reconstruction of the scale armour used by Frankish warriors in the 9th–10th centuries. During the reign of Charlemagne, those Franks who owned large amounts of land were required to own body armour; a chainmail tunic was recorded as selling for 12 *solidi*. According to records from the 860s the price of a Frankish helmet was six *solidi*, a valuation suggesting that they were made of metal rather than leather (Coupland 1990). (DEA/C. BALOSSINI/ Getty Images)

his captured livestock to form an impromptu rampart, the stench of the dead livestock halting the cavalry advance and prompting the Franks to open negotiations instead.

Known as the Treaty of Saint-Clair-sur-Epte, the subsequent agreement between Charles the Simple and Rollo is given little detail by the surviving chronicles. We do know that it occurred in a year when the Franks faced renewed assault from multiple directions: the Magyars had crossed Bavaria, invaded Swabia and Franconia and were threatening Burgundy for the first time while the Fatimids, the major Islamic power on the Franks' southern flank, commenced their conquest of Sicily and began raiding the southern Italian coast. On 24 September in that momentous year, the East Franks elected Conrad I (861–918; r. 911–18) as the successor of Louis the Child (893–911; r. 900–11), marking a decisive step away from Carolingian hegemony in what would become Germany.

The Treaty of Saint-Clair-sur-Epte was supplemented by a second settlement made in 921, following Duke Robert of Neustria's defeat of a Viking army in the Loire Valley. Robert was the younger brother of Odo, erstwhile count of Paris and king of West Francia; he had played an important part in the defence of Paris in 885–86 and pledged allegiance to Charles the Simple, fighting to defend the realm against the Northmen in his capacity as *dux Francorum* (Duke of the Franks). Robert would himself become king of West Francia, being crowned at Rheims on 29 June 922 only to die just under a year later; he was succeeded by his son-in-law, Rudolph, who reigned until 936.

As with the terms of the Treaty of Saint-Clair-sur-Epte, the 921 settlement entailed the baptism of the Viking leaders in Paris, signifying their submission to the West Frankish king. In practice the Vikings continued to follow their pagan beliefs alongside their Christian undertakings, likely seeing no contradiction in hedging their bets as the balance of power between royal authority and local opportunities ebbed and flowed. It is likely that Rollo understood the Treaty of Saint-Clair-sur-Epte to require him to resist the depredations of other parties of Northmen who might seek to raid the area around the Seine. In the event, Rollo proved to be a loyal ally of Charles the Simple even after the latter's deposition in 922, rather than transferring his allegiance to Robert and Rudolph (Collins 1999: 377). The foundations were therefore laid for the full participation of the Northmen in their territories around the Seine, which came to be known as Normandy, in the dynastic politics of West Francia as it became France.

Analysis

How can we gauge whether the Vikings succeeded on their own terms? In the absence of Viking accounts, the motivations for their assaults across the Frankish realm have been contested among scholars. Although some commentators have suggested that the Vikings' pagan beliefs spurred them to attack Christian religious centres, this is not borne out by the sources; although individual monks did die at the hands of the raiders, the majority appear to have escaped, leaving only those determined to sacrifice their lives (Coupland & Nelson 1988: 7).

Frankish religious texts help us to understand the raiders' intentions (Coupland & Nelson 1988: 8). While nobles and other prominent individuals could be seized and exchanged for a ransom, other captives were taken to slave markets across the known world. The slave trade was a major part of economic life in the Viking Age and fortunes could be made from selling captives in a variety of locations, not least in Scandinavia itself.

Unlike in other places, such as Russia and England, it appears that settlement was not the aim of the Vikings operating in Francia. The Viking leaders were nobles searching for plunder to finance their activities at home. Archaeological finds in Denmark suggest increased efforts to cultivate the land during the 9th century. With plunder and slaves gained in Francia, a Viking warrior could improve his chances of competing successfully in ongoing power struggles in his homeland. Even in Normandy, the only part of Francia where a Viking settlement survived and thrived, the newcomers left fewer traces than in the English Danelaw across the Channel (Coupland & Nelson 1988: 9). The Viking settlement in Normandy was founded by Rollo, who had converted to Christianity and cultivated a fruitful working relationship with neighbouring Frankish rulers; it is striking just how successfully the Northmen were assimilated into Frankish political and military life over the ensuing decades, with their fundamental views of how society should operate being very similar to those of their Frankish counterparts (Coupland & Nelson 1988: 10).

The Frankish armies that fought in Charlemagne's offensive campaigns against the Lombards, Saxons and others during the closing years of the 8th century had gained much experience in fighting a variety of foes in many different settings. During the drawn-out Saxon Wars, the initial pitched battles and sieges had given way to the pursuit of dispersed opponents amid the marshes and forests of Saxony, with the Franks unleashing a brutal combination of forced conversion, hostage-taking, deportations and reprisals. The men who led Frankish forces in the efforts to resist the Vikings had probably gained substantial military experience during Charlemagne's wars, and formed networks with other junior commanders. The Frankish armies that faced Scandinavian marauders varied greatly in their size, composition and purpose, but it is reasonable to assume that they drew – at least in theory – on the Frankish military elite's hard-won military expertise accumulated during many decades of successful campaigns across Europe. Why, then, did their efforts against the Vikings frequently fail?

One reason lies in the dilution of focus and effort among the Frankish forces. It is important to remember that while seeking to counter the Viking threat the Frankish kings continued to prosecute wars against other peoples beyond the Frankish frontier, such as the Bretons, and were repeatedly caught up in the confused civil wars and revolts plaguing Francia during and after the reign of Louis the Pious. The forces available to combat the Vikings were inevitably limited by these competing demands for military resources.

A second reason lies in the conduct of the elusive opponents the Franks faced. Ultimately, although the Franks were formidable in pitched battles and siege warfare, they were confronted with a highly mobile enemy who rarely allowed himself to be trapped. British historian Simon Coupland notes multiple Frankish victories over the Vikings (2004: 66–67), but even an outright victory was ephemeral as the defeated Northmen would simply retreat, regroup and try again somewhere else. As Coupland concludes (2004: 69), the only way for Frankish rulers to secure a long-term solution to the Viking menace was to offer the Northmen lordship of lands within the Frankish realm – as did Louis the Pious with the county of Rüstringen in Frisia, Lothair I with Walcheren, and Charles the Simple with the area around Rouen that came to be known as Normandy – or tribute, in exchange for the Viking leaders' promise to commend themselves to a Frankish overlord, convert to Christianity and refrain from raiding Frankish territory.

Although the payment of tribute has been heavily criticized as a short-term response that actually spurred further Viking raiding, the evidence suggests that Charles the Bald succeeded in ridding his kingdom of those Viking contingents whom he paid, and the sums required were raised without forcing his regime to debase the coinage or push the Frankish people into hardship (Coupland & Nelson 1988: 7). Importantly, though, the decentralized nature of the raiding parties meant that it was difficult for Frankish leaders to negotiate with one high-profile opponent and thereby dispel the Viking threat altogether; this fragmentation among the Vikings meant that it was often more fruitful for the Franks to pay one group of Northmen to fight another, or to police a particular region on the crown's behalf.

Although modern historians have blamed Frankish ineffectiveness in the face of the Viking threat on failures of military organization and the royal

Picture stones such as this one from the island of Gotland in Sweden populated the rural landscapes of Viking Age Scandinavia. While the Franks relied upon their clergyman and scholars to record much of their history, the Vikings erected stones detailing important scenes of warfare and conflict. This stone may denote a ship of Odin carrying souls into the afterlife or a warband of raiders travelling to the location of their next expedition. As a society that thrived on oral traditions and storytelling, the Vikings passed down their memories through verbal communication and often picture stones such as this one. (DEA/G. DAGLI ORTI/De Agostini via Getty Images)

host's sluggish tempo of mobilization, the local forces comprising the *lantweri* were often highly motivated and more than capable of defending their homes, given the right leadership and the opportunity to prove themselves in battle. Rather than competing for resources and prestige, local military efforts complemented the royal host's bids to track down and defeat the Vikings (Coupland & Nelson 1988: 5). Crucially, it was the Franks' lack of suitable watercraft that meant they could not take the fight to the Northmen's island fastnesses, thereby surrendering the initiative to the Vikings and leaving swathes of Frankish territory open to surprise attack (Coupland 2004: 69–70).

Frankish authors of the 9th century offered additional reasons for the Franks' inability to overcome the Northmen, such as cowardice among Francia's military leaders (Coupland 2004: 70). The sources tell us a different story, however, with many such leaders taking the Viking threat seriously and in some cases giving their lives in defence of Frankish territory. Other contemporary writers blamed internal political division; this was undoubtedly a factor that significantly aided the Northmen. Coupland notes (2004: 70) that Lothair I actively encouraged the Vikings to attack West Francia in a bid to undermine his rivals' rule.

It is hard to avoid the conclusion that the Frankish warrior caste were as concerned about losing their monopoly on military and political power as they were about the Viking threat. Charles the Bald insisted that fortifications built without his permission should be torn down, in a bid to assert royal power in the face of local initiatives; even so, by the 890s, there appears to have been a profusion of local fortresses as individual communities tried to protect themselves against the raiders (Coupland & Nelson 1988: 6–7). Even those Frankish local forces who successfully defended their homes against the Vikings in the absence of aristocratic or royal leadership could find their lords turning on them rather than the raiders, as the *Transsequanani* found to their cost in 859; their decision to take their defence into their own hands meant

A selection of coins from the Cuerdale Hoard, found in Lancashire, England, in 1840. Portable wealth such as silver and other precious metals was frequently given to Viking marauders in exchange for promises of peace. After a profitable season of raiding and the extraction of tribute, a Viking warrior could hope to return home in Scandinavia and use his newly won fortune to support his own political and military ambitions. While Francia was divided by a series of civil wars, Scandinavia remained a collection of petty kingdoms constantly at war with one another for much of the Viking Age. (CM Dixon/Print Collector/Getty Images)

they were viewed as a threat to the Frankish order, and they were massacred (Coupland 2004: 54).

Ultimately, it was the Vikings' tactics, especially the mobility afforded to them by way of their longships and their establishment of island bases and fortifications, which gave them the ability to continue their activities in Francia in the teeth of Frankish resistance. At the same time, Frankish internal political struggles – on occasion, spilling over into outright civil war – proved crucial in undermining the Frankish forces' efforts to counter the Scandinavian threat.

It is instructive to compare the Frankish experience of conflict with the Vikings with that of their Anglo-Saxon neighbours. Engagements between the Vikings and Anglo-Saxons were not much different from those that occurred in Francia. Important towns and coastal villages were burned and sacked by small companies of Viking marauders. On the battlefield, the Anglo-Saxons relied on spears and shields just as the Vikings (and Franks) did. Full-scale battles seldom occurred in Anglo-Saxon England, just as in Francia. The most significant contrast between Viking activity in England and Francia was the advent of the Great Heathen Army, a collection of warriors from across Scandinavia that invaded much of England.

Regarding measures taken against the Vikings by Anglo-Saxons, British historian Gareth Williams states that the first responses were reactive. The Anglo-Saxons mustered forces to combat the Vikings or negotiated terms when victory appeared unlikely (Williams 2017: 26). The Anglo-Saxon victory at Edington in 878 won Alfred of Wessex sufficient time to develop a network of fortified towns – burhs – which aided the resupply of his forces while restricting the ability of his opponents to gather provisions (Williams 2017: 26). This measure of containment, deliberately employed to neutralize the Vikings' greatest asset – their mobility – would be effective in helping defeat the Great Heathen Army, the largest Viking force known to have existed.

Aftermath

The agreement reached by Rollo and Charles the Simple in 911 heralded the waning of the Viking Age in West Francia. This was not a result of enhanced royal authority among the Carolingians and their Capetian successors; rather, it was because the local magnates had moved to take their defence into their own hands, refortifying towns and building castles across their domains as royal authority weakened (Haywood 2016: 107–08). The building of fortifications proved effective in countering different types of raiding, whether Viking, Magyar or Saracen, but the key question was how to raise and maintain the forces necessary to garrison such works. It was expensive to raise armies large enough to garrison these fortifications effectively – after all, if left ungarrisoned or poorly prepared, they could fall into enemy hands and actively impede local efforts to resist the raiders – and so local communities had to be persuaded, not browbeaten, into paying for their own defences, and serving in their lord's forces (Davis 1988: 163–64).

In this work of persuasion the lords of smaller territories were much better placed than the emperor of a vast territory such as Charlemagne's realm; they could inspire and lead their followers in person, and were seldom so far away that they could not lead defensive efforts in person. Unlike a notional overlord in a palace far away, these local magnates could respond rapidly and effectively to threats to their domains, aided in their endeavours by the continued rise to prominence of the fully armoured horsemen who would dominate European warfare in the High Middle Ages.

Around the year 1000, Christianity began to spread rapidly in Scandinavia. In addition to this, the emergence of proper kingdoms and 'nation-states' as opposed to the tribal clan politics of the Early Middle Ages transformed the political landscape of Northern Europe. The Scandinavians were active well into the 11th century but fought in more formal, unified armies. Indeed, the same peoples who had raided the Christian Franks of the 9th century would turn their attention to attacking pagan peoples even more isolated

The royal monogram of Hugh Capet (c.939–96), who succeeded the last Carolingian monarch, Louis V (c.966–87; r. 979–87), as the king of the West Franks (r. 987–96); the Capetian dynasty would rule France until 1328. (DeAgostini/Getty Images)

Reconstruction of the Viking barracks at the fortress of Trelleborg, west of Slagelse on the Danish island of Zealand. The stronghold consisted of a circular rampart and two paths that cross in the centre, creating four equal segments, each occupied by four Viking longhouses. The fortress is believed to have been built by Harald 'Bluetooth' Gormsson, king of Denmark and Norway (r. c.958–c.986), as the Viking Age was ending in Francia. (Werner Forman/Universal Images Group/Getty Images)

from the European mainstream than the far reaches of Scandinavia during the Northern Crusades of the High Middle Ages.

The downfall of Carolingian rule in East Francia occurred in 911 with the death of Arnulf's sole legitimate son, Louis the Child. While Charles the Simple had no likelihood of succeeding to the throne of East Francia, as the only living adult Carolingian, he set his sights on the land between the two kingdoms – Lotharingia. Charles took over the middle Frankish kingdom with the support of the Lotharingian elite and his wife, Frederuna, who was a member of the nobility. Charles was deeply invested in the new land acquired for his kingdom, though members of the nobility felt that this was at their expense (Collins 1999: 395). Subsequently, in 922, a large portion of the West Frankish elite rebelled against him. As a primary source for Viking activity in East Francia, the *Annals of Fulda* do not discuss events occurring after the year 901, by which time the Viking Age was gradually reaching a discernible end.

Instead of the Vikings, a new threat emerged for East Francia as the 10th century dawned. A steppe-nomad confederation, the Magyars (referred to as *Ungari* or Hungarians in East Frankish sources), wreaked havoc and destruction through their raids against the realm. By the 940s, however, the Magyar threat was receding, prompting efforts on the part of the East Frankish monarchy to seek to impose its authority on the kingdom's regional magnates (Collins 1999: 395).

BIBLIOGRAPHY

Medieval sources

While there are more medieval sources than can be listed in full in the confines of these pages, here is a brief overview of key sources providing evidence for the Viking Age in Francia. Note that all of these sources are written from a Frankish perspective; no equivalent Scandinavian sources survive.

The *Annales regni Francorum* (Royal Frankish Annals), composed at the Frankish royal court, cover the years 741–829 and are considered to be the single most important source for the reign of Charlemagne. As is the case with many annalistic records, the *Royal Frankish Annals* provide a brief and rather dry narrative, leaving the reader uninformed on many topics related to military history.

The *Annales Bertiniani* (Annals of Saint-Bertin), covering the years 830–82, are the primary narrative source for the Carolingian realm of the 9th century. This source was produced at the imperial palace of Louis the Pious in the 830s, first by Prudentius, bishop of Troyes, until his death in 861, and then by Hincmar, archbishop of Rheims, until he died in 882. The *Annals of Saint-Bertin* are unique as they relay the personal voices of two different authors and contain detailed information on the reign of Charles the Bald. No other source provides as much evidence for Viking activity on the European continent.

The *Annales Fuldenses* (Annals of Fulda) are the primary narrative source written from a perspective east of the Rhine. The *Annals of Fulda* cover the period from the last years of unified Frankish rule under Louis the Pious to the end of Carolingian kingship in East Francia with the accession of Louis the Child in 900. Valuable details concerning the battle of Louvain in 891, as well as other encounters between Viking and Frankish warriors, are given in the text. The account of the battle of Louvain is especially descriptive, providing the speech given by King Arnulf to the royal host just before combat against the Vikings.

The *Annales Vedastini* (Annals of Saint-Vaast) were written by an unknown monk of the Benedictine abbey of Saint-Vaast near Arras in Flanders (Dunphy 2010: 95). Covering the history of West Francia during the years 874–900, the *Annals of Saint-Vaast* do not relay much information beyond that concerning events occurring within the western realm. This source is significant for its account of the Norman invasions.

The *Annales Xantenses* (Annals of Xanten), covering the years 790–874, provide a monastic account of important events in Carolingian Francia (Dunphy 2010: 94). Named the *Annals of Xanten* on account of the author's description of destruction at the abbey of Xanten, the sole manuscript copy was found in the library of Robert Cotton (1571–1631), a British antiquarian and Member of Parliament.

The *Bella Parisiacæ urbis* (Wars of the City of Paris) of Abbo of Saint-Germain-des-Prés is a Latin poem about the Viking siege of Paris in 885–86. Abbo's dramatic eyewitness account vividly portrays the unrelenting attacks of the Vikings, the dogged resistance of the defending Frankish warriors, and the general terror of the Parisians under attack.

An illustration accompanying Psalm 44 in the *Utrecht Psalter*, a 9th-century masterpiece of Carolingian art. (Universal History Archive/Universal Images Group via Getty Images)

Modern works

Adrien, C.J. (2018). 'L'Histoire des Vikings à Noirmoutier' ('The History of the Vikings in Noirmoutier'). Available at https://cjadrien.com/2018/10/08/vikings-a-noirmoutier/ (accessed 14 November 2020).

Anonymous (2019). 'An Account of the Siege of Paris, 885–886', in A.A. Somerville & A.R. McDonald, eds, *The Viking Age: A Reader, Third Edition (Readings in Medieval Civilizations and Cultures)*. Toronto: University of Toronto Press: 239–42.

Apelblat, Mose (2016). 'Was Leuven Founded by Vikings? Lost History and Legend'. Available at https://www.brusselstimes.com/news/magazine/39054/was-leuven-founded-by-vikings-lost-history-and-legend/ (accessed 14 November 2020).

Bachrach, B.S. (2001). *Early Carolingian Warfare: Prelude to Empire*. Philadelphia, PA: University of Pennsylvania Press.

Bowlus, C. (1978). 'Warfare and Society in the Carolingian Ostmark', *Austrian History Yearbook* 14: 3–26.

Collins, Roger (1999). *Early Medieval Europe 300–1000*. Second edition. Basingstoke: Macmillan.

Cooijmans, C. (2015). 'The Controlled Decline of Viking-Ruled Dorestad', *Northern Studies* 47: 32–46. Available at 10.17613/nq2e-bk29

Cooijmans, C. (2020). *Monarchs and Hydrarchs: The Conceptual Development of Viking Activity across the Frankish Realm (c.750–940)*. Abingdon: Routledge.

Costambeys, M., Innes, M., & MacLean, S. (2011). *The Carolingian World (Cambridge Medieval Textbooks)*. Cambridge: Cambridge University Press.

Coupland, Simon (1990). 'Carolingian Arms and Armor in the Ninth Century', *Viator: Medieval and Renaissance Studies* 21: 29–50.

Coupland, Simon (1991). 'The Fortified Bridges of Charles the Bald', *Journal of Medieval History* 17.1: 1–12.

Coupland, Simon (2003). 'The Vikings on the Continent in Myth and History', *History* 88.2: 186–203.

Coupland, Simon (2004). 'The Carolingian Army and the Struggle against the Vikings', *Viator: Medieval and Renaissance Studies* 35: 49–70.

Coupland, Simon (2007). *Carolingian Coinage and the Vikings: Studies on Power and Trade in the 9th Century*. Farnham: Ashgate.

Coupland, Simon & Nelson, Janet (1988). 'The Vikings on the Continent', *History Today* 38.12: 1–13.

Dunphy, Raymond Graeme (2010). *The Encyclopedia of the Medieval Chronicle*, Volume I. Leiden: Brill.

Ferguson, Robert (2010). *The Vikings: A History*. New York, NY: Penguin Books.

Friðriksdóttir, J.K. (2020). *Valkyrie: The Women of the Viking World*. London: Bloomsbury Academic.

Ganshof, F.L. (1970). *Frankish Institutions Under Charlemagne*. New York, NY: W. W. Norton & Co.

Haywood, John (2016). *Northmen: The Viking Saga, AD 793–1241*. New York, NY: Thomas Dunne Books/St. Martin's Press.

Hedeager, Lotte (2012). 'Scandinavia before the Viking Age', in S. Brink & N. Price, eds, *The Viking World*. Abingdon: Routledge: 11–22.

Hjardar, Kim & Vegard, Vike (2016). *Vikings at War*. Oxford & Philadelphia, PA: Casemate.

MacLean, Simon (1998). 'Charles the Fat and the Viking Great Army: The Military Explanation for the End of the Carolingian Empire', *War Studies Journal* 3.2: 74–95.

MacLean, Simon (2017). *History and Politics in Late Carolingian and Ottonian Europe: The Chronicle of Regino of Prüm and Adalbert of Magdeburg*. Manchester: Manchester University Press.

McKitterick, Rosamond (1995). *The Carolingians and the Written Word*. Cambridge: Cambridge University Press.

McKitterick, Rosamond (1999). *The Frankish Kingdoms under the Carolingians*. New York, NY: Pearson.

Nelson, Janet L. (1991). *The Annals of Saint-Bertin (Ninth-Century Histories)*. Manchester: Manchester University Press.

Nelson, Janet L. (1997). 'The Frankish Empire', in Peter Sawyer, ed., *The Oxford Illustrated History of the Vikings*. Oxford: Oxford University Press: 19–47.

Nelson, Janet L. (2020). *King and Emperor: A New Life of Charlemagne*. London: Penguin.

Nicolle, David (1984). *The Age of Charlemagne*. Men-at-Arms 150. London: Osprey Publishing.

Nicolle, David (2005). *Carolingian Cavalryman AD 768–987*. Warrior 96. Oxford: Osprey Publishing.

Noble, Thomas F.X. (2009). *Charlemagne and Louis the Pious: Lives by Einhard, Notker, Ermoldus, Thegan, and the Astronomer*. University Park, PA: The Pennsylvania State University Press.

Parker, Philip (2014). *The Northmen's Fury: A History of the Viking World*. London: Jonathan Cape.

Price, Neil S. (1989). 'The Vikings in Brittany', *Saga-Book* XXII: 319–440.

Reuter, Timothy, ed. (1992). *The Annals of Fulda (Ninth-Century Histories)*. Manchester: Manchester University Press.

Roesdahl, Else (2016). *The Vikings: Third Edition*. New York, NY: Penguin Books.

Scholz, Bernhard W., trans. B. Rogers (1970). *Carolingian Chronicles: Royal Frankish Annals and Nithard's Histories*. Ann Arbor, MI: University of Michigan Press.

Shippey, Tom (2018). *Laughing Shall I Die: Lives and Deaths of the Great Vikings*. London: Reaktion Books.

Turner, Danielle (2017). 'The Viking Sieges of Paris: Brilliant Warfare or Pragmatic Decision?', *Medieval Warfare* VII.1: 26–33.

Welsh, William E. (2017). 'Laying Waste to Everything: Viking Tactics in West Francia', *Medieval Warfare* VII.1: 16–19.

Williams, Gareth (2017). *Viking Warrior vs Anglo-Saxon Warrior: England 865–1066*. Combat 27. Oxford: Osprey Publishing.

Williams, Gareth (2019). *Weapons of the Viking Warrior*. Weapon 66. Oxford: Osprey Publishing.

Winroth, Anders (2012). *The Conversion of Scandinavia: Vikings, Merchants, and Missionaries in the Remaking of Northern Europe*. New Haven, CT & London: Yale University Press.

The 10th-century Fyrkat Viking ring fortress near the town of Hobro, Denmark. While not as permanent and robust, Scandinavian encampments in Francia were traditionally of a semicircular design. Although the Franks were renowned practitioners of siege warfare, the Vikings were simply too mobile – and too wary, retreating to their ships or carefully chosen river islands between raiding forays – to be caught and besieged by their Frankish adversaries. The sources relate that the Franks were able to lay siege to the Northmen at Angers in 873, Asselt in 880 and the Hesbaye region, between the Meuse and the Scheldt, in 885 (Coupland 2004: 65). The imposition of a blockade, denying the defenders supplies and reinforcements, worked to the Franks' advantage at Angers and in the Hesbaye, although in the former encounter the Franks themselves experienced shortages and sickness, according to Regino of Prüm. The siege of Asselt resulted in an unsuccessful Frankish investment (see page 64), but the reason for this apparent loss is unclear. (DEA/A. DAGLI ORTI/Getty Images)

INDEX

References to illustrations are shown in **bold**.
References to plates are shown in bold with
caption pages in brackets, e.g. **54–55**, (56).

Aachen, Viking attack on 5, 64
abbeys/monasteries, Viking attacks on 4, 5, 11,
    15, 19, 34, 48, 62, 64, 65, 66, 77
Alemannia 5, 38, 60, 68
Angers, Frankish siege of 14–15, 29, 48, 59, 79
Anglo-Saxon forces/weapons 23, 27, **61**, 74
Aquitaine 4, 5, 9, 18, 34, 40, 52, 61, 66
archers/archery: (Viking) 28, 29, 32, 46;
    (Frankish) **54–55**, (56)
armour: (Viking) 7, 12, **12**, **13**, 24, 25, **42–43**,
    (44), **54–55**, (56); (Frankish) **16**, **17**, 18, 26,
    42–43, (44), **54–55**, (56), 70, **70**
Arnulf of Carinthia 16, 62, 66, 67, 68, 69, 76
Asselt, Frankish siege of 62, 64, 79

Ballon, battle of 48, 50
Bavaria 5, 8, **9**, 47, 60, 66, 69, 70
Bordeaux, Viking raid on 48, 53
Bouin, Viking raid on 34, 40
bows and arrows: (Viking) 28, **46**, 65, 67;
    (Frankish) 18, **18**, 26, **54–55**, (56)
Bretons 9, 10, 19, 30, 34, 48, 59, **63**, 66
    Breton-Viking forces 48, 50, 58
    Bretons, revolt of 6, 50, 52, 58, 72
Brissarthe, battle of 48, 58–59
Burgundy 5, **9**, **63**, 66, 69, 70

Carloman I, king of the Franks 5, 8, 60, 68
Carloman II, king of West Francia 61, 62
Charlemagne, king of the Franks 4–5, 5, 6, 8,
    10, 15, 18, 19, 21, 25, **25**, 26, 31, **31**, 32,
    33, 34, 36–37, 38, 39, 41, 61, 64, 67, 72
Charles, king of Provence 48, 59, 53
Charles the Bald, king of West Francia 15, 18,
    19, **19**, 22, 25, 38, 44, 45, 46, 47, **47**
    campaign against Vikings 19, 25, 29, 30,
        48, 52, 53, 57, 59, 60, 61, 72, 73
    cooperation with Vikings 57, 58
Charles the Fat, king of the Franks 60, 61, 62,
    64, **64**, 65–66, 68
Charles the Simple 62, 66, 69, 70, 72, 75, 76
Chartres, Viking siege of 62, 69–70
coinage **6**, 20, **26**, **31**, 72, **74**
Condé/Courtrai, Viking raids on 64

Danelaw **63**
Danevirke 8, 34, 36
Denmark, territories of 8, **8**, **9**, **35**, **63**
    civil wars in 10, 34, 37
    Frankish expeditions into 34, 36, 38–39
Dorestad, Viking raids on 8, 32, 34, **35**, 37,
    40–41, **42–43**, (44), 44
Dyle River, Viking raids along 62, 67, 68

Flanders, Viking raids in 48, 50
Fontenoy, battle of 46, 48, 52
Frankish armies: cavalry forces 12, 16, 17, **18**,
    22, 26, 27, 58, 62, 68, 69; composition/size/
    shortcomings 18, 72; raising/mobilization of
    18, 22, 25–26, 75; royal host 15, 16, **16**, **17**,
    22, 23, 25–26, 34, 36, 37, 48, 57, 58, 59,
    72–73; scouts 29, 67; tactics 29–30
Frankish Empire 4, 5, 8, **9**, **35**
    civil wars/dynastic wranglings 6, 23, 34, 38,
        41, 44, 45, 46–47, 48, 50, 52, 53, 57, 60,
        66, 69, 72, 73, 74
    defences, bridges/rivers/towns 18–19, 32,
        34, 36, 37, 39, 44, 46, 48, 52, 57–58,
        62, 64, 65, 73: *lantweri* 4, 15, 25,
        30, 73

defences, coastal 15, 19, 26, 31, 32, 36, 39,
    40, 46: coast guard 4, 15, 18, 25, 34, 39
partition of kingdoms 47, 48, **49**, 53,
    60–61, **63**, 66, 76
Frankish fleet (rivercraft/ships) 8, 15, **15**, 18,
    30, 32, 34, 36–37, 44, 73
Frisia **9**, 15, 30, 32, **35**, 53, 72
    Viking raids along 8, 15, 18, 34, 36, 37, 39,
        40, 44, 48

Garonne River, Viking raids along 50, 52
Godfred, king of the Danes 21, 31, 34, 36, 38
Godfrid (Viking leader) 48, 53, 62, 64, 68
Great Heathen Army 23, 61, 74

Halfdansson, Harald 'Klak' 34, 37, 38, 39,
    48, 53
Hamburg, Viking sacking of 48, 50
Hastein (Viking leader) 58, 59
Hedeby trading centre 28, 34, **35**, 36
helmets: (Viking) 7, **12**, **13**, 24, **42–43**, (44),
    54–55, (56); (Frankish) **16**, **17**, 18, **22**, 26,
    42–43, (44), **47**, **51**, **54–55**, (56), 70
Hemming, king of the Danes 34, 36, 37
Horik I, king of the Danes 50

Isles-lès-Villenoy, fighting at 18, 48, 57
Italy, Kingdom of 8, 48, **49**, 53, 59, 60, 61,
    63, 66

javelins/lances (Frankish) **22**, **42–43**, (44),
    54–55, (56), 66
Jengland, battle of 48, 50, 58
Jeufosse, Vikings at 25, 48, 53, 57

Le Mans, sacking of 48, 58
Lindisfarne, Viking raid on 5–6, 8
Loire River, Viking raid on 18–19, 32, 57
Loire Valley, Viking raids in 30, 34, 50, 53,
    58–59, 70
Lombardy/Lombards **9**, 72
Lothair I, king of Middle Francia 22, 34, 25,
    38, 39, 44, 45, 46, 47, 48, **51**, 53, 72, 73
Lothair II, king of Lotharingia 18, 48, 53, 59
Lotharingia 18, 48, **49**, 53, 59, 60, 66, 76
Lothbrok, Ragnar (Viking leader) 48, 50, 52
Louis II, king of West Francia 60
Louis III, king of West Francia 29, 61, 62
Louis V, king of West Francia 75
Louis the Blind, king Provence 66
Louis the Child, king of East Francia 68, 70, 76
Louis the German, king of East Francia 22, 34,
    38, 44, 45, 46, 47, 48, 57, 59, 60, 64
Louis the Pious, king of the Franks 8, 10, 19,
    26, 32, 34, 38–39, **40**, 41, 44, 45, 46, 50,
    52, 53, 59, 60, 72
Louis the Stammerer, king of West Francia
    61, 62
Louis the Younger, king of Saxony/Bavaria
    15, 48, 53, 60, 62, 64
Louis the Younger, king/emperor of Italy 59
Louvain, Viking attack on 12, **12**, **13**, 14, 16,
    16, **17**, 26, 62, 64, 67–68

Magyars (*Ungari*/Hungarians) 68, 70, 75, 76
Melun, fighting at 48, 58
Meuse River, defensive measures on 32, 66, 69
Montfaucon, battle of 62, 66

Nantes, Viking attack on 34, 48, 50, 53
Neustria 5, **9**, 40, 70
Noirmoutier, Viking raids on 4–5, **5**, 34, 11,
    25, **35**, 50
Nominoë (Breton ruler) 48, 50
Normandy, Vikings settlement in 69, 70, 71

Odo, king of West Francia 19, 58, 62, 65, 66,
    67, 68, 69, 70
Oissel, Frankish siege of 48, 57
Oscar (Viking adventurer) 52, 53

Paris, Viking sieges of 19, 29, 48, 50, 52, 57,
    62, **62**, 64, 65–66, 70
Pepin I, king of Aquitaine 34, 38, 46
Pepin II, king of Aquitaine 46, 48, 52, 53
Pepin the Hunchback 32, **33**
Pepin the Short, king of the Franks 8
Perche (forest of), fighting in 48, 53
Pont-de-l'Arche, defences at 18, 48, 57, 58
Provence 5, **9**, 48, **49**, 53, 59, 66

Ragnold, duke of Le Mans 62, 64
Ranulf I, duke of Aquitaine 59, 66
Remich, battle of 62, 64
Reric, Viking attack on 34, **35**, 36
Rheims, Viking sacking of 64, 70
Rhine Delta, Vikings in 34, 44
Robert the Strong 48, 58, 59, 65
Rollo (Viking leader) 62, 69–70, **71**, 75
Rouen, fighting at 10, 50, 62, 64, 69

Saucourt-en-Vimeu, battle 29, 62, 64
Saxons/Saxony 8, **9**, 34, 38, 47, 64
Scheldt River/Valley, Viking activity 64
Seine River, Vikings raids along 18, 22, 23, 30,
    34, 39–40, 48, 50, 52, 53, 57, 58, 62, 64,
    65, 66, 69, 70
Seine Valley, Viking activity in 48, 58, 61, 62,
    69, 70
shield bosses: (Viking) **12**, 24, **28**, **32**;
    (Frankish) 16
shields: (Viking) 7, 11, **12**, **13**, 27, 32, **32**,
    42–43, **54–55**, (56); (Frankish) **16**, **17**,
    18, **22**, 26, 30, **42–43**, (44), **54–55**, (56)
siege equipment/warfare: (Viking) 27, 29, 65,
    79; (Frankish) 59, 65, 66, 72, 79
Sigfrid, king of the Danes 31, 53, 62, 64,
    65, 68
spears/spearheads: (Viking) 7, 21, 27, 28, **28**,
    38, **38**, **54–55**, (56); (Frankish) **16**, **17**, **18**,
    26, **30**, 66, **66**
standard-bearers/standards (Frankish) **22**, 68
swords/sword blades: (Viking) **12**, **13**, 20, **20**,
    21, **21**, 36, **42–43**, (44), **51**, 65; (Frankish)
    17, 18, 21, **25**, 26, **42–43**, (44), **54–55**,
    (56), **57**

Thimeon, battle of 62, 64
Toulouse, Viking attack on 48, 50, 52
Trier, Viking attack on 62, 64

Viking armies: assembly/gathering of 20:
    captives/hostages/slaves, taking of 37, 44,
    57, 59, 71; conversion to Christianity 50,
    69, 70, 71, 72, 75; encampments 10, 14, 15,
    25, 48, 50, 53, **54–55**, (56), 57, 58, 62, 64,
    65, 67, **76**, **79**: islands, use of 14, 15, 18,
    30, 48, 50, 53, **54–55**, (56), 57, 58, 59, 74;
    plunder, taking of 10, 11, 25, 37, 44, 62,
    67, 71; tactics/formations 27–29, 37, 50,
    74; tribute, payment of 19, 34, 36, 37, 48,
    52, 57, 58, 62, 64, 66, 72, **74**; versus Vikings
    19, 48, 72
Viking fleets 15, 23, 44, 57
    longships, use of 4, **5**, 11, 14, **14**, 18, 32,
    32, 34, 36, 39, **42–43**, (44), 47, 48, 50,
    52, **52**, **54–55**, (56), 65, 66, 68, **73**, 74

Weland (Viking leader) 48, 57